FREDERIC WHITAKER

BAROQUE FACADE

FREDERIC WHITAKER

by Janice Lovoos

NORTHLAND PRESS, FLAGSTAFF, ARIZONA

CONTENTS

ILLUSTRATIONS

For almost forty years the name
Frederic Whitaker and the word *watercolor* have been synonymous.
So closely allied is the artist to his medium that one can scarcely think of the New
England-born painter without calling to mind his aquarelles: artistic records of places
he has visited, their landscape, architecture, people, a flowing panoramic observation
of life seen through his eyes.

If it is watercolors that have brought him the widest reputation, they are only
one facet of a long and unique career. He has distinguished himself as a designer,
craftsman, silver manufacturer, and writer. In view of his success in both creative
and business enterprises, one might well ask, "What sort of man IS this?"

Once you meet Frederic Whitaker you are not likely to forget him. He walks taller
than his exactly-six-foot height. Wise blue eyes evaluate you thoughtfully from under
heavy brows. He gives you a firm handshake.

A stray lock of hair falls over one eye at a rakish angle. He glances at you somewhat owlishly over heavily rimmed glasses with a secret kind of smile that seems intent on some mischief — perhaps a story he is about to share with you. The image of Senior Statesman vanishes; he is a perennially youthful, very large elf.

A basically shy man he may tell you that he has never yet achieved completely one single goal. But Frederic Whitaker has the unmistakable appearance of a man who has, indeed, attained his goal in life.

What a contrast to this distinguished figure the *boy* Frederic must have been! A small, insecure ragamuffin who was usually left to his own devices to roam the streets of a shabby neighborhood.

"Cause and effect are inseparable. What we are and do as children clarifies the reason for adult activities," Whitaker once told the press in an interview. His life bears out his statement.

Frederic Whitaker was born on January 9, 1891, at 28 Ackerman Street, Providence, Rhode Island. His father, Edward Reginald Whitaker, and his mother, Ada Hands, were both natives of Birmingham, England — as were their parents before them.

In the throes of a rapidly advancing industrial age the grandparents had prospered, successful in business, well adjusted to their social environment. Frederic's grandfather, Richard Whitaker, was a manufacturer of silverware and metal products. Thomas Hands, Ada's father, was a cabinetmaker of some reputation. But such affluence was not to be the lot of the younger Whitakers starting life in a new land.

Edward and Ada had been childhood sweethearts but young Edward, "Ted," was itching for adventure. At twenty-one he was off to find it in military service as a common soldier in the army commanded by Lord Roberts, famous in history as "Little Bobs" — in charge of the British forces during the Burmese War, and in India. Ted was a bandsman, playing French horn.

Throughout their nine-year separation the two young people faithfully corresponded. When Ada's father died, she and her mother sailed to America to make their home with Ada's elder sister in Rhode Island.

By this time Ted was ready to put down roots. When he returned to England to find his former sweetheart gone, he lost no time getting to America. He called at her home in Providence on a Sunday evening, and the following Wednesday they were married.

"Their marriage," Fred contended, "brought together for life as mismatched a couple as anyone could imagine." There had not been sufficient time for the surprised Ada to discover that Ted, now thirty, was not the same boy she had known in his teens.

During his roustabout years in the army Ted had acquired a taste for drink and although it was never for anything stronger than beer, the amounts required to appease his thirst were enormous. His wife was a total abstainer. With such opposite views it would have been surprising had all gone smoothly. Fred can still recall the constant bitter quarreling between his parents. Friction notwithstanding, five sons were born within the first eight years of their stormy life together. They arrived in the order named: Richard, Roland, Frederic, Harry, and Victor Herbert. Roland survived only a few days after his birth.

Luckily Ted had picked up enough knowledge of silversmithing and metalsmithing at his father's plant to land a job with the Gorham Company. Wages were modest, $18 to $20 per week for a sixty-hour week. The Whitaker family of six lived in what would now be called "substandard" housing. They were constantly being exposed to inadequate heating and plumbing, to faulty bathroom facilities, if such could be dignified by the name.

"During the winter months," Fred pointed out, "it seemed that I was never warm, that being cold was an unavoidable condition. It never occurred to me that *anyone* could be warm in winter!"

Years later he learned that it was possible to be comfortable in zero weather, provided one was properly clothed; inadequate clothing was the basis of the problem. Wearing apparel was usually made by his mother. An uncle's old trousers were cut down to make knee-pants for the four boys. Ada Whitaker was an avid bargain hunter. She needed to be. Shoes were purchased solely with regard to price. "Our *feet* had to adjust to the *shoes!*"

Along with the scorching heat, summertime brought on an avalanche of cockroaches; in winter the children suffered from chilblains. They were often hungry. "Pop's habit" was making heavy inroads into the family budget. "Pay day was on Wednesday but occasionally we ran out of food by Tuesday. We went through these days with literally nothing to eat though nearly always we had tea in the house."

Present-day welfare workers would certainly classify the small Whitakers as underprivileged children. Yet Fred remembers little talk of poverty. "I am sure we were as well satisfied with life as the pampered children of today." Had Fred or his brothers asked how they endured such hardships their answer, in effect, would have been, "Doesn't everybody?" They didn't consider themselves poor. Nor did they hold the shortcomings of their parents against them.

Despite his father's weakness, Fred had great admiration for him. "He was an unusually intelligent man, physically as strong as a lion. He was a skilled craftsman and, aside from the drinking bouts, he was a real hard worker. My mother was a wonderful woman even if she was the world's worst cook. In retrospect, she was just beaten down by adversity."

If poverty had an advantage it was in making Fred aware of the value of things. "I had to learn to live with very little money." It also made him ingenious.

What the Whitaker boys possessed beyond bare necessities had to be earned. With his younger brother Harry — the only brother to whom Fred was ever close — he would walk along the sandy banks of the Quinnipac River to pick watercress which they sold Saturday on the main street of Wallingford at five cents a bunch. The boys' intake amounted roughly from sixty cents to seventy-five cents. At an open plain where skeet shooters gathered, they found thousands of empty shotgun shells. They would gather them, burn out the paper castings from their metal bases and sell the scrap brass to junkmen. Other jobs included working as a golf caddy at ten cents an hour and delivering the *Wallingford News* at eighty cents per week. Harry was hired by Fred on a fifty-fifty basis to help deliver, on foot, several thousand throwaway papers. That gave each boy forty cents take-home pay.

Not everyone had a Christmas tree. Certainly not the Whitakers! One year Fred's longing for a tree of his own was so great that he and his brother Harry walked to a nearby woods where they cut down a sizeable pine branch. Not knowing the characteristics of a pine from a fir they hopefully dragged it home, only to find it already shedding. Their mother would not tolerate it in the house so they rooted it in the ground outside and decorated it with wooden spools.

Spools were, in fact, important in creating toys, as were string, old boxes, and cartons. The "make-it-yourself-or-do-without" rule, mandatory in Fred's youth, made him extremely facile with his hands. It undoubtedly influenced later inventions such as the first Talking Book (1929) and disc wheels, as the first metal wheels for automobiles were called.

He had no "planned campaign of invention" — ideas came to him casually, usually so far ahead of his time that he did not reap the monetary benefits. Yet they appeared on his drawing board years before they appeared on the commercial market or had been discussed publicly by anyone.

"As a mechanical draftsman," he explained, "I worked things out on paper and discussed them with authorities of the day. In each case the 'authorities' dismissed the ideas as impractical. As I had no intention of developing these things myself, I let them lapse." (In the case of the Talking Book, R.C.A., in New York, was the authority.)

Muzak was another idea which Fred discussed with the American Telephone Company in Providence "years before Muzak was ever hear of." The use of metal panels to fill in the wall space between the iron girders of tall buildings, to replace the standard use of bricks for this purpose, was another of his ideas.

But his "correspondence with President Farrell of U.S. Steel brought me the customary response: that the advantage of such metal panel construction had not yet been demonstrated." Of course, it is now in common use.

Fred is philosophical about it. "In each case it was gratifying later to see these advances brought out by experts. Incidentally, most of Leonardo's inventions never went beyond the drawing board."

If the Whitaker's economic situation never seemed to change, their residences did. Up until the time Fred was married at age twenty-one, they moved fourteen times. Twice, because of his father's work, they journeyed to other cities, once to Philadelphia, then to Wallingford, Connecticut when Fred was eleven years of age. They lived there four years.

At age fourteen no boy should stay in school! That was Ted Whitaker's opinion as well as that of many other parents of that day who were in comparable strained circumstances. Two weeks after Fred's fourteenth birthday he went to work for the M. Backes Company in Wallingford. At this fireworks plant his job was running the machine that produced giant firecrackers.

One of the procedures was to make paste out of flour and water, achieved by inserting the pipe into the mixture and blowing live steam through it. The mixture had to be cooked until it became very thick, until "the rising bubbles burst languidly."

Unsupervised on the second day of his job and with scanty instruction the day before, Fred undercooked the paste and POW! Ten thousand tubes — the casings for fireworks — blew up! This unfortunate happening did nothing to endear this kind of job to young Fred and when an opportunity to work for the R. Wallace and Sons Company (also in Wallingford) presented itself, he lost no time in accepting it.

These early encounters with the business world were followed by a series of various jobs, each one supplying the boy with a different type of knowledge. Among the jobs were those of press hand, metal stamper, machine operator in a textile mill, errand boy, and maker of curtain rods. Later he became a mechanical draftsman, cost estimator and factory paymaster.

Although the salary earned as errand boy, at two times in his early career, was negligible, the experience proved invaluable. In what other capacity would he have had entrée to every department of the complex silver business. Fascinated by all he saw, Fred became acquainted with the various artisans and, being of an inquiring nature, never hesitated to ask questions.

In Providence, the Braitsch Company specialized in manufacturing handles for canes and umbrellas. The cane was then a mark of distinction, more so if it happened to be a gold-headed cane. Canes were also made of rolled gold and silver. When Fred began work there as a chaser's apprentice things looked promising. His work (chasing) was to emboss designs on metal with steel punches. His wages were to be $3.00 a week. But when his second pay envelope was opened, it only contained $1.75. It was explained that the deduction would be taken from each pay check during his four-year apprenticeship. Then it would be returned in a lump sum at the end of the four years!

"No one expected high wages in those days — but $1.75!" His father instructed him to quit the job. "So I left Braitsch to let them get along as best they could without me." Putting metal tips on shoelaces at the Elmwood Mill was not as creative, but it was more profitable. Pay was good — $6.00 per week.

Although Fred had drawn since he could hold a pencil, he had never given serious thought to pursuing art as a career. In retrospect, after seventeen years of writing monographs on successful artists, illustrators, and painters he was surprised to learn that nearly all of them knew from childhood the eventual careers they wanted to follow.

"While I was always interested in pictures and I used to practice drawing at every opportunity, I never dreamed I might one day reach a position as exalted (as I thought of it then) as that of an artist. I did, however, hope that some time in the future I might achieve *something* but without ever pausing to decide what *that something* might be."

Fred was a natural designer and it was design that determined his career. Born into a family of creative craftsmen, exposed to it from childhood, watching designs 'grow' from paper to drawing board to finished product, plus his own natural bent, how could he escape it? And if Fred was not certain about his talent, Ted Whitaker was. He was thoroughly convinced that his son was a born artist and as such, his budding genius should be recognized.

When Fred was in his teens a brand of cigarettes called Sweet Caporal appeared on the market. Each pack contained one or more reproductions of flags of various countries. They were collected and "swapped" as photos of picture stars were at a later date. Fred copied the reproductions with colored crayons in minute detail. He even learned to draw some of them from memory.

Impressed by the fidelity of the work, Ted was quick to display his son's talent whenever he had a captive audience. Company had only to stop by the Whitaker home and soon he was saying, "Fred, draw a flag!" The boy obediently complied. When the drawing was finished it was displayed by the father with great pride.

On such occasions Fred played it safe. "I drew only those flags requiring the least ingenuity. *I* realized my shortcomings even if *Pop* did not."

But the elder Whitaker was determined that Fred must be successful in the art career that was inevitable. A man with considerable gifts of persuasion, he tackled John Gabriel Hardy, head of the design division of the W. J. Feeley Company which manufactured religious articles of metal. His approach was direct and to the point.

"I have a smart kid," he told him, "who is a wonder at design. Why don't you give him a job in your department?" The outcome of their conversation was that Fred was hired as Hardy's assistant. He had just turned sixteen. If this seems young to assume a job of responsibility it was indicative of a pattern. A wage earner in his teens assumes a responsible attitude. Everything seemed to start early with Fred.

This job was unlike any other he had experienced, just as Hardy, London-born and a cultured gentleman, was unlike any other man Fred had ever met. "He had more to do with the crystallizing of my outlook than anyone else — even my own father." The new job changed his outlook and gave his life a definite direction.

With Hardy, Fred had to learn by "observation and emulation." Because Hardy assumed "everybody knew everything" — therefore he need not explain or demonstrate how things were done — it was often difficult for the embryo designer, especially when he was called upon to execute work that required knowledge far beyond that of his limited experience.

For example, his very first assignment was to "Make an accurate, finely detailed pen-and-ink drawing, in actual size, of a thirty-inch, elaborately decorated ostensorium." Frederic had no idea what Hardy was talking about. It was left to Owen Logan, the other draftsman in the design room, to enlighten him as to the purpose of an ostensorium and the form the drawing was to take. An ostensorium, or monstrance, is a transparent or glass-faced shrine used by the Roman Catholic Church, in which the consecrated host is presented for the adoration of the people, either when carried in a procession or when exposed on the altar. It is placed in a stand that is usually made of precious metal, sometimes lavishly jewelled.

It was also on this job that Hardy gave him the first and last definite instruction he was to receive in his seven-year stay at Feeleys. Fred had been struggling with an acanthus leaf cusp and his drawing resembled a lot of seaweed.

"Hardy seated himself in my chair and said, 'This is really a very beautiful leaf. Notice that it goes like this. . . .' And with the greatest of ease drew the thing exquisitely. I could have cried with mortification and frustration. However, once I grasped the fundamentals, I knew that art was my metier."

Fred's job at Feeley's was to create unique ideas for special customers. This included preparing the "show drawings" which had to be done to scale, meticulously and accurately.

These careful renderings broadened his interest in design. But more than that, from executing them he gleaned a tremendous knowledge of watercolor techniques, to the point where he became expert in handling the difficult medium. In fact, the education he was receiving daily at Feeley's was building a strong basis for his future as an artist.

During his stay at the Feeley plant Fred designed and supervised the making of literally hundreds of pieces in gold, silver, brass, and bronze. From the artistic point of view he was unaware of the value of things he was producing, unacquainted with publicity or promotion. So he kept no personal record although well-known priests, bishops, archbishops, and cardinals were the recipients of his creative efforts.

Presentations of his pieces were made to Pope Pius X and Benedict XV. Publicized or not, the name Frederic Whitaker was becoming known.

Several years earlier he had been granted a State Scholarship, available at age sixteen, to attend night classes at the Rhode Island School of Design where he studied life drawing for four years. This was more or less the extent of his formal art education. Now, in his new enthusiasm, he took an inexpensive course in pen-and-ink drawing. On the night he attended school, he used the one hour between his work and classes to pour over books in the art department of the Providence Public Library.

He had always been an avid reader and because of the inevitable book-in-hand, was referred to by schoolmates and his family as the "bookworm." When he started bringing books to read at the dinner table, his mother at first forbade the practice. Finally, realizing it was hopeless, she accorded him the privilege.

Books laid out his code of ethics. "The Ellis and Alger books made a terrific impression on me," declared this artist whose own success story somewhat parallels that of a Horatio Alger plot. "But my parents had set before me, by teaching and example, a strict standard of morality and probity. The books that I read (such as those by Alger) with their emphasis on honorable and industrious behaviour, impressed me forcibly. Much later I realized the purpose of these books was not just to entertain, but to build character.

"So, I think it was at an early age when I began to see things from the other fellow's point of view and to be considerate of his feelings. I always have had little regard for deadbeats, four-flushers, goldbrickers and all those who demand much for doing nothing. I expected to work hard."

Now, with a goal in view he considered this renewed period of study and learning as good training and "It gave me an understanding of the value of time that I have never forgotten. Even today I am irked by situations whose hours do not produce."

Wages were turned over to his mother, but out of his small allowance he indulged in two luxuries. Once a week he bought himself a bag of chocolate-covered almonds and a copy of *Life* magazine — not the *Life* magazine we know today, but a humorous publication filled with illustrations by his favorite artists: Charles Dana Gibson, Orson Lowell, and Gordon Grant. In later years he counted Gibson and Grant among his many artist friends, but at that time they were romantic and famous figures whose pen-and-ink techniques he admired and studied.

The Feeley plant was owned by William J. Feeley, whose father had established it in 1870. It was the first company of its kind in America to produce Catholic religious articles from metal. This type of merchandise had heretofore been imported from Europe. When Fred had worked there for two years the ownership was transferred to a Mrs. McElroy, who immediately put her son Robert in charge of the plant.

Bob McElroy was a likable young man who came to a difficult job with no special training for it, and little business experience. Being socially inclined, the first change he made was to partition off a section of the designing room where tea could be served every afternoon. The word got around in short order; heads of the various departments usually found an excuse to join him for "tea at four."

Fred was fond of the amiable Bob, even though the latter's goal in life seemed to be having fun, and Fred, at the other end of the pole was, as usual, immersed in work. For various reasons (some of them personal) Feeley and Hardy, the designer, did not share this fondness for the new manager. One day when Hardy refused to apologize to a customer, a Monsignor, whom young McElroy felt the designer had insulted, a heated argument ensued. In the middle of it, Hardy resigned his position and left in a huff. Fred was immediately put in charge of the design department. He had two other designers, a draftsman and a modeler, or sculptor, as his assistants. He was now twenty-three!

McElroy's lack of fitness for his job led to increasing absenteeism. It was no surprise that after attempting to run the business in such a haphazard manner, they were forced to liquidate.

The old maxim, "It's an ill wind that blows no good," was an apt one when the Feeley Company closed its doors and, indirectly, opened up a whole new career for Fred Whitaker.

In a final goodwill gesture to a few loyal employees, McElroy offered them the opportunity of buying the company's merchandise at inventory prices. Taking the suggestion of McElroy's right-hand man, Fred and the office manager Bob Mangan, bought a large quantity of rosaries at a very low price.

With samples in hand they departed for New York and Boston and quickly returned with a $4,000 profit. Fred, it seems, has never been content to stick his fingers into only one pie, nor had his friend Bob Mangan. The idea of establishing their own business often entered into their conversation.

Elated over the results of their first selling venture, they registered at the Providence City Hall as a partnership, taking the name of The Esmond Company. Shipping was done from the Feeley plant, billing from their own Esmond Company. Money owed for the merchandise was to be paid to Feeley's when they, in turn, were paid.

In order to provide an address, they rented a room in downtown Providence.

Photograph of colored drawing of gold chalice, set with jewels. Height, 9 inches.

Photograph of colored drawing of sanctuary stand lamp of bronze, plated with gold. Height, 60 inches. An example of designs and show drawings made by Frederic Whitaker during his earlier days of metalware designing and manufacturing.

Their next selling venture concerned a large supply of glass beads. Providence was the heart of the jewelry business (as it is today) and it was a simple matter to find out which New York buyers were in town and at what hotels they were stopping.

They selected the name of a man who had visited the Feeley plant several times. He agreed to come to their 'showroom' at three o'clock the same afternoon. Imagine his surprise when he walked into a room devoid of everything except the samples of beads displayed on the window ledge! Not even a chair to sit on!

The man's sharp eyes sized up the situation. "How much for the lot?"

Summoning all his courage, Fred blurted out. "$4,300!" He knew it was a low price. "$4,000!" the man countered.

Fred felt sure of his sale. "$4,300 is the bottom!" He was certainly ready to drop the price if necessary.

It wasn't necessary. Without another word the man left the office.

Crestfallen, Fred regretted to report failure to his partner. But, two heads being trickier than one, they figured out a surefire way to win. Mangan would now call the prospective buyer and, as Fred's "superior," would accept his lower bid. The sale was made.

Having tasted success, they were bitten by the 'selling bug'. They would go into the mail order business!

Both young men needed to work to support their project. Fred took a job with the Gorham Company, at that time the largest business of its kind; Gorham's kept forty designers and modelers busy turning out merchandise. At Gorham's, during the day, Fred was involved in the designing and making of bronze tablets.

Fred explained the nature of their activities: "Mangan, sculptor Aristide Clansfarari, Charles Williams, a specialist in plaster casting, and I started making *objets d'art* from a mixture of plaster of Paris and glue which sets extremely hard. These objects — candlesticks, plaques in the style of Andrea Della Robbia, and novelties of comparable type — were finished in subdued colors and gold, with a fine patina."

Working nights, Fred designed the articles, Clansfarari made the models. Williams worked full time doing the actual manufacture of the pieces and Mangan, who was then a traveling salesman working mostly in New York, carried their samples as one of his sidelines.

For such an ambitious project they needed a factory. For a few dollars they rented an old cottage in South Providence. Knowing that plaster "makes an awful mess" they considered the place ideal. "It was *so* decrepit it was ready for the demolition squad."

One room was chosen for the casting department, others were filled with racks for hanging and drying the casts, another for coloring and finishing, one for storage and still another for shipping.

"Charlie reported that the place was rife with bedbugs. During off moments he would range about with hammer, bestowing on them their *coups de grace.*"

Their products were given a cordial reception by buyers and they soon found their way into the best New York stores. Fred retains a fatherly affection for these early pieces, and even now has some of them in his possession. "I am still impressed with their excellence," he says.

Despite this encouragement on the part of buyers, they made no money on their venture and closed the factory.

Although Mr. Goldman, the landlord who lived close by, was at liberty to inspect the premises at any time, he never availed himself of the privilege until he came to collect the final rent.

He had been apprised of their plans and methods before production had begun. But apparently he had not understood them in their full meaning. For when he saw the interior of his cottage for the first time, he went into a mild state of shock. Seeing the stained racks in the bedrooms, the floors and walls covered with plaster, all he could do was to clap his hands to his head and moan over and over, "Oh, my poor house! My poor house!" Then he started to cry.

If no money was made, some knowledge was gained through this venture.

"Here we learned," Fred recalls, "the truth that all business men know and that others will not believe, namely that it costs more to *sell* an article than to *make it,* and that selling prices must necessarily be calculated in the light of that fact."

Fred had always been extremely shy and sensitive and had never paid any serious attention to girls. Not because he didn't like them — quite the contrary! He admits being 'madly in love' with two young girls in the first and second grades. But he knew he would bungle it if he tried to be friendly, and so they were never aware of his feelings.

In high school he was self-conscious to the point where he would blush if a member of the opposite sex spoke to him. That included women teachers. He was twelve years old, the youngest student in the school, but because he was large for his age, girls would sometimes try to wangle him into walking home with them.

None were very successful in carrying on a conversation with the tongue-tied boy.

These attempts did nothing to build his morale. "To me they seemed like full-grown women. Imagine a gawky twelve-year-old with a seventeen-year-old girl!"

He tried to explain his feeling further. "Perhaps my position then and now, has been unusual. I wouldn't say that I had an inferiority complex. In the beginning I was too young to know about that. But I did have a strong feeling or appreciation of class or rank.

"I considered my own position in the world to be a normal one, but that anyone even slightly above that status, such as a labor gang foreman, to use a modest example, was a very important person and entitled to special deference. I believed that improving one's station was an extremely difficult business."

With work, however, it was a different story. Once Fred started on a project, he could completely lose himself in the doing of it. Work-oriented from boyhood he became a keen observer of life, a 'doer' instead of a thinker. Yet, he felt a paucity of social graces and disclaimed having any of them.

In his late teens he decided to improve his image by taking lessons in ballroom dancing. On several consecutive nights he was "pushed through three or four dances by the robust attendants." That ordeal over, he was supposed to ask a girl to dance with him. But the old bogey-boo, timidity, again had him by the tongue. He lost his nerve! Not until he was in his twenties did he take another stab at the art of Terpsichore; it was around his dancing period that romance entered his life. It appeared one day quite unexpectedly in the form of Marie Tiedge, his junior by a few months. Fred and Marie "fell promptly in love."

Marie was his first girl, Fred was her first beau. Before they were twenty-one, they were engaged. Before their twenty-second birthdays, they were married. That was in 1912. Fred was making $18 per week. Neither he nor his young bride understood the first thing about what marriage entailed. If possible, they knew even less about one another.

"Undoubtedly my own naiveté and ignorance of women was a contributing factor to our trouble. Had I been a 'man of the world' I might have been able to tactfully dominate the situation."

Marie Tiedge had been raised in a German family in which education of the female members was concentrated on cooking and housekeeping. Her practical training was put into good use when she married Fred. During the economic struggle of their first years of marriage, she carefully balanced budgets, kept homes and wardrobes in perfect order.

Three children were born to this union: a son, Frederic Herman, a second son, Teddy, who died in infancy, and a daughter, Marion, who was later to become Mrs. Donald K. Thurston.

Marie was a devoted mother. In fact, to her, *family was all,* to the exclusion of almost any other friends who Fred felt might enrich their cultural lives. She could appreciate Fred as a good father, a hard-working provider, but beyond these family ties, no real empathy ever existed between the two. To understand Fred as an artist, was simply beyond her comprehension. Despite this lack of encouragement, Fred's status as a designer was on the rise.

In 1921, he was making $250 per month, when he left the Gorham Company for the greener fields of Tiffany. If in 1972 that seems like a small salary, in 1921 it was a handsome fee, indeed, and the fact that he was paid twice a month by *check* was equally impressive. Workers in those days were paid each week in cash.

It was not so much the money involved as the prestige of Tiffany that made every designer in the country eager to be associated with its famous name. Fred's salary at Tiffany's was small, $50 a week, but even at that time it was twice what the average craftsman earned. To Fred, it meant the added expense of living in New York, while his family remained in Providence. In order to maintain two households, he lodged at the Y.M.C.A. He ate his meals at cheap restaurants. There was nothing left over for entertainment. To Fred, whose chief drive had always been in the direction of work, this did not pose a problem. He was glad for the evenings in which he spent most of his time making designs for the following day. He was eager to prove to Arthur Barney, head designer at Tiffany, that he had not misplaced his judgment in hiring him.

About once every two weeks he returned to Providence for the weekend, to see Marie and the children. This proved too costly to become a regular practice. Apartments in New York averaged $24 per room, per month. No matter how he tried to stretch the money, it never seemed enough to house Marie, the children, and Marie's mother in New York.

It was not likely that a larger salary would have solved anything. Marie did not care for New York. In fact she refused to live there. To add to his frustrations he picked up an infection in his chin which required daily medical care for several weeks. It was at this discouraging period that Bill Peck, formerly plant manager at the Feeley Company, paid him a visit.

Peck was a hardheaded business man who pointed out to Fred that more money was to be made in selling than in designing — in any business. Would Fred be interested in selling for his company, The Cathedral Art Metal Company? It sounded like a solution to his needs and the disheartened Fred jumped at the chance.

In addition to selling the merchandise that Peck produced, church furniture and small religious articles, Fred also designed some pieces which were sold to the general trade. With his usual awareness, Fred began to visualize some plans of his own.

In that same year, with a capital of $2,500 he started his own manufacturing business, making religious wares from his original designs. Not only was Fred a fine designer, he had the uncanny faculty of knowing what would sell. Once again Robert Mangan became his business partner. They called it The Mangan Company and hired girls to assemble the merchandise. The new company became the talk of the religious goods industry. Many tried to emulate them. The beauty of Fred's designs, however, kept them leading the parade.

They used a unique approach in selling to priests and other church members. In those days salesmen calling on the Church trade went about their jobs in an almost unctuous manner. They wore the traditional black clothing deemed necessary to call on the clergy. These two youthful entrepreneurs shed the funereal attire and offered them merchandise at reasonable prices through spirited advertising such as department stores might use. This was an unheard-of practice. The clergy was delighted to buy at reduced prices — just like anyone else.

Of his eleven years in The Mangan Company, Fred spent probably one-third of his time on the road, selling to Catholic priests and nuns in the various convents. At one time or another he made calls on virtually every convent and Catholic institution east of the Mississippi.

Many asked, "How was it possible for you, a Protestant and Freemason, to sell religious articles to the Catholic clergy and those of the Catholic religion?" Fred never experienced any difficulty. To offset any possibility of misunderstanding right from the start, it was his custom to wear his Masonic pin.

Fred recalls that during his thirty years in business he "enjoyed the personal friendship of hundreds of priests and nuns, and I am proud to say that I am still in correspondence with a number of them."

Although Fred had designed and sold rosaries of every description, even today he refers to an incident in Mexico at this time as the "rosary-making deal."

His talents for turning a creative idea into a salable product were unique. But even good ideas, as he had already learned from his own Talking Book and disc wheel experience, could be ahead of their time. So now, in 1941, bright as the promise of an exciting and lucrative venture seemed, the "rosary-making deal" turned out to be an expensive fiasco.

Here is his own account of what happened: "Our supply of European, very cheap rosaries having been shut off by the war, in 1942 I conceived the idea of setting up a rosary-making establishment in Mexico. In Mexico City I acquired an interpreter, Eduardo Gonzales, and showed the people how to make the things we wanted and left Gonzales as our agent.

"His duty was to ship us all the rosaries he could have made for which he was paid fifty cents per gross. We paid six dollars per gross for the rosaries. This may seem a very low figure but actually it was double what we had previously paid for comparable merchandise in Europe. Before long every American religious goods distributor was using Mexican-made rosaries.

"If I remember rightly, the duty into the United States was forty-five percent ad valorem. In importing it has always been understood that the value of a thing is what one has to pay for it, but after the rosaries had been coming in for a year, the Customs Department decided, arbitrarily, that the value was $9.50 per gross. On my personally protesting to the New York office of the U. S. Customs, I was told to get out or be thrown out. Bureaucrats!

"While in Mexico I became acquainted with the most beautiful silver jewelry, which at that time was practically unknown in the United States. Thinking that it would be used to replace the then unprocurable Czechoslovak costume jewelry that had been so popular, I purchased $15,000 worth from several factories for a tryout.

"Surprisingly, the American department stores would have none of it. Most of our stock was literally given away. Today Mexican silver is in brisk demand here. These transactions introduced me to Mexico, which I have visited a score of times, passing through virtually every one of its states."

Never does he underestimate the value of his selling experience: "I can think of no training that will teach one more about human nature, about business, about what makes our economy function, and about getting along with others, than that of selling — and by selling, I do not mean the taking of orders brought to one, but traveling about and rooting out business. . . the intelligent salesman has both feet on the ground — the attitude of virtually everyone who has ever really done anything for this world."

Two years later Fred took a sabbatical, presumably to design greeting cards and other items that would utilize his various skills. These things he did, and successfully. But his mind never ran on just one track.

The following year he purchased the Foley and Dugan Company which also manufactured religious wares. In 1941 he bought the G. H. Seffert Company that produced ecclesiastical materials and for a while, managed the two firms. Both were moribund when he bought them. With the quality of his work, plus his New England sagacity, both firms again became financially solvent. Insofar as his work was concerned, Fred now seemed to be in a winning cycle. But when it came to a closer, happier relationship with Marie, the effort was always an uphill pull. Never did they succeed in reaching any kind of a plateau of understanding. To Fred, one of the most deflating incidents, one which started to write finis to their mismatched union, occurred in the thirties.

From an eccentric uncle, Marie had inherited a fourteen-room house on the outskirts of Providence. Fred, who had never stopped dreaming about a life which he could share with other creative people, now saw in the old house in its rather romantic setting, a golden opportunity. How he hungered for friends with comparable interests! What an ideal place for creative people to gather together at intervals to share ideas and discuss their mutual problems! Why, it would attract interesting artists, writers, educators, musicians, thinkers in all walks of life, for miles around!

Much of the cultural life at that time centered around the Providence Art Club. If Marie attended the functions at all, she did it with the greatest reluctance. To her, artists were people not to be trusted. Weren't they all parasites? She would have no part of such a hairbrained scheme. When she closed the door, once and for all time, on that opportunity, Fred was shattered. He needed friends and he would have them.

Marie, on the other hand, realized that art was becoming increasingly important to Fred, more demanding of his time. She actually feared for their future. How, she reasoned, could anyone seriously consider art as a livelihood? But Fred was determined to paint, and in an atmosphere of peace and quiet. He set up a studio in back of the office at the plant.

"Eventually my routine became what now appears to have been a ridiculous one. Rising at six-thirty I made my own breakfast and left home six miles from town before the others were awake, reaching the office before eight o'clock for a preview of the mail. Lunch and dinner were eaten in town and then I would return to the studio to paint until around ten or ten-thirty, arriving home around eleven o'clock when the others were already asleep. Sunday morning and evening meals were the only ones taken with the family. There could be only one ending to such a schedule."

In 1940 the Whitakers separated. Two years later, although still living apart, they had not yet divorced.

Throughout these years of designing, selling, building, and rebuilding businesses, Fred had never stopped painting. The day would come, he felt sure, when he could devote his entire time to it. Already he was making inroads into the world of art with showings of his watercolors.

In 1943, on the occasion of his first one-man exhibit at the Ferargil Gallery in New York, Emily Genauer, well-known art critic, singled it out for a favorable review in the *New York Telegram*. The following statements are quoted from that article:

"Whitaker, for a practicing silversmith, for anyone, in fact, is singularly free and spontaneous in his work. Maybe it derives from the strong rhythm of his design . . . possibly it is due to their atmospheric quality. At any rate, they speak eloquently of his technical skill, of his imagination, and of his poetic, romantic feeling toward nature."

But Miss Genauer's appreciative nod to Fred's talents was not the only piece of good fortune that fell his way on that February in 1943. On St. Valentine's Day Fred stopped by the Ferargil Gallery. Also visiting was a young lady who had come to see his exhibit. The owner of the gallery introduced them. She looked up at him with the kind of "smiling Irish eyes" tenors are prone to celebrate in song. She was small and feminine. Dark hair framed a sensitive face whose every expression suggested a happy nature. She was Eileen Monaghan, a successful artist in her own right, twenty years his junior. They had so much to say to one another, so much to share, that they continued their conversation over lunch. When they finally said good-bye, they had agreed on a future date for dinner.

Both of them were involved in businesses outside of their weekends dedicated to painting. Fred was still engaged in business in Providence, Eileen was art editor of a trade magazine. They began to enjoy sketching trips together, although due to gas rationing, trips were short. It was on a weekend spent with Eileen's sister in Pleasantville, that they realized their relationship was evolving into something more than merely "good friends."

Marie had been quite unhappy about the status of "separation" between herself and Fred. Despite the continuing lack of understanding and the ever-widening breach between them, she resisted officially ending their ill-favored marriage, especially when she learned that Fred was serious in his intentions about someone else.

In desperation Fred finally sought a divorce in Mexico and consequently he and Eileen were married in Arlington, Virginia, on December 11, 1950. Because the validity of Mexican divorces had not been tested, Fred's attorney suggested a second ceremony. After three years of marriage the Whitakers were married a second time, this time in New York.

It was also during Fred's period of great productivity in which he was developing as a painter, that his finest piece of art metal work was produced. Archbishop Rummel described it as "the most beautiful ostensorium in existence and the most costly vessel ever made in this country." This is undoubtedly true when one considers the fact that it was set with $100,000 worth of diamonds and other precious stones from a collection of jewelry donated by New Orleans parishioners. The donations included everything from old eyeglasses to exquisite diamond brooches.

On the following pages Whitaker has described how the project unexpectedly got under way and how, in detail, it was accomplished.

THE OSTENSORIUM

In March of 1938, a Mr. Bernard, of the retail jewelry firm of Bernard and Grunning of New Orleans, called on me in my Providence office without previous notice, saying he had come from Louisiana to persuade me to design and make the magnificent ostensorium that Archbishop Rummel required for the great Congress to be held in September of that year. The deadline for submission of design entries was only ten days away from the date of our conversation. In view of his eloquence and the special trip he had made I agreed to handle the job. He, it appeared,

*Ostensorium, or monstrance, made entirely of 14-karat
gold and platinum, set with many hundreds of precious stones.
Height, 42 inches. Weight, 27 pounds. Designed and made
by Frederic Whitaker for Archbishop Rummel,
of New Orleans. Used, in Benediction, by Cardinal Mundelein,
of Chicago, at the Eighth Eucharistic Congress, 1938.*

was intimate with the authorities of the New Orleans Archdiocese, and he came prepared with a great amount of data bearing on the desires of the Archbishop.

The ostensorium was to be designed in the Italian Renaissance style. It was to be made of solid fourteen karat gold and platinum, as large as practical, for Exposition of the Host at Benediction in the open before myriads of the faithful, and its weight was not to be over twenty-five pounds so it could be elevated by the Cardinal. The design was to be rich in symbolism and to include innumerable emblems.

The finished work did include more emblems, coats of arms, figures, precious stones, and allegorical representations than in any other work in precious metal I have ever seen, whether contemporary or of the past. One of my stated conditions was that I could reject anything not conducive to an artistic whole.

I must quote one extreme example of the kind of symbolism someone had favored. According to Bernard, "They would like to have around the base four or five medallions depicting scenes important in the history of Louisiana. One should be that of The Battle of New Orleans showing Jackson's forces, behind a rampart of cotton bales, holding off the British.

"The convent of the Ursiline Sisters [the first religious order to be established by the French in Louisiana] was close to the battlefield, and during the battle, the Sacred Host was exposed on the tabernacle of the Chapel to invoke divine aid for the American arms.

"So if you will make a bas relief of the battle, showing also the chapel through which the monstrance with Host can be seen on the tabernacle, that would be splendid for one of the medallions."

Now, I ask the reader to visualize all this, compressed within the circular border of a three-inch disc, and to calculate just how much could be seen on the monstrance on the altar.

But at least the suggestions gave me plenty of material with which to work. So, telling my staff that I would be absent a week and was not to be summoned on any pretext, I went home to work and within a week a full-sized colored design of the forty-two inch monstrance had been worked out, together with detailed drawings of the individual parts from which the modeler (sculptor) and the many workmen — silversmiths, chasers, metal spinners, engravers, enamelers, some setters, metal molders, jewelers and others — could estimate the time for their services, and their value.

Shortly afterwards came telegraphic confirmation of our having won the competition by unanimous vote of the judges over a field of twenty-four competitors, including two from Europe. Stipulation was made that delivery of the finished monstrance must be made by the end of August.

To help finance its construction, collections had been carried out in the various branch parishes of Louisiana, of old gold and precious stones, eyeglass rims, gold dentures, and jewelry of all kinds. Some donors insisted that their exquisite diamond brooches, earrings and the like, were to be mounted intact on the sacred holder of the Host. I ruled these stipulations out in the knowledge that otherwise the piece would simply constitute a vulgar display of wealth, for I had had opportunity to study similar situations on many earlier occasions.

All jewelry had been taken apart in New Orleans; the diamonds, rubies, emeralds, and other stones were kept separate and, on order of the church authorities, the gold was melted and forwarded to me in several enormous lumps. This gold then had to be refined and alloyed to fourteen karat quality.

Here we ran into a lot of trouble. It will be recalled that President Franklin D. Roosevelt devalued the dollar by increasing the value of gold from $21 to $35 per ounce in 1933, first calling in all gold money, and had ruled that the government's guarantee to redeem its bonds and gold notes in gold was no longer valid, and had made it unlawful to own gold money or to handle gold without a permit. Our refiner pointed out that the Archbishop unknowingly had violated federal law in having the gold jewelry melted and that he, the refiner, could not touch the metal until the prelate's position had been clarified and we had received an official permit to use the gold. The Archbishop's office, attempting to clear the issue with Federal authorities, was soon bogged down in a mesh of bureaucratic tape and probably would still be arguing the matter had not heroic measures been adopted.

Meanwhile I had been working on the necessary scores of individual detailed working drawings for the various artisans; the sculptor had made his many models, hundreds of additional diamonds had been bought, to say nothing of similar numbers of opals, garnets, and other stones. The spinners had made their chucks, the drawings had been made for etching the many coats of arms, the diemaker had finished his dies for repetitive parts, and many other workers were involved in the various processes required. In fact everything possible was done short of working out the actual ostensorium. After many communications with the Archbishop, I was forced to notify him that unless the gold permit arrived by a certain date there would be no ostensorium for the Eucharistic Congress.

At that time Jim Farley, a staunch Catholic, was Postmaster General under Roosevelt. Calling him on his phone, the Archbishop explained the predicament and indicated that he depended on Farley to get the gold permit. It reached us within hours, and the ostensorium was finished on time. The Archbishop described it as the most beautiful and most expensive piece of religious goldsmithing ever executed in this country.

During the progress of this work, I was asked by the Archbishop to design and make six candlesticks and the crucifix for the outdoor altar of the Congress. These measured four and six feet respectively, as I remember them. They were of massive design and made of bronze.

Before going to New Orleans, the monstrance was displayed in the window of the leading dealer in objets d'art of Providence, the Tilden Thurber Company, under police guard, and the viewing throng was so enormous that Westminster Street, the main thoroughfare of the shopping district, was packed from one side to the other during the day so that traffic had to be rerouted. Even the Railway Express Company sent an armed guard with the shipment by air to New Orleans.

The ostensorium is now kept with the treasures of the Cathedral of St. Louis in New Orleans.

The artist who has never experienced *teaching art* is a rarity. In 1958 Fred and Eileen Whitaker had a go at it. Hiring a large room in downtown Norwalk, Connecticut, overlooking the head of the river, they opened classes in drawing and watercolor painting, charging five dollars per student for each three-hour lesson. Eighty percent of the students were women, wives of doctors, lawyers, industrialists, legislators, and other citizens of affluent Fairfield County.

"We found this work to be most enjoyable," Fred comments, "and, as is often true, we learned a great deal more than some of our students. But after six years of teaching, Eileen's itchy foot began leading us away on three-month trips to Mexico, the American Southwest, Europe, and Canada." Feeling that their erratic schedule was unfair to students, they discontinued their formal teaching in 1964.

At the beginning of the same year they were each granted a Fellowship by the Huntington Hartford Foundation at Pacific Palisades, California. Eileen's project was to explore the possibilities of the new acrylic polymer artist's paint. Fred devoted the time to writing his second book. In 1957 *Whitaker on Watercolor* had been published by Reinhold Publishing Company.

"We stayed there for three months. Each couple, or individual, was given a cottage with a studio. Ours was one designed by Frank Lloyd Wright, Junior."

The Huntington Hartford Foundation offered an idyllic situation for the creative person. Lunches were delivered to each cottage daily so that the Fellows could continue their work without interruption. Breakfasts and dinners were served in the main building.

"The general conversation took place at these two times, plus the evenings for those who wished to remain. Because of the heterogeneous character of the *fellow* set-up, very few controversial subjects were discussed during the conversation periods."

One could, however, express personal opinions when fellow visited fellow in private cottages during the evening. Fred soon discovered he was not the only one writing a book. Dorothy and Mark Van Doren occupied a cottage nearby and it was through these nocturnal gabfests that they came to know well, and admire, the distinguished pair.

On one occasion the four of them were discussing writing. Fred asked Mark Van Doren. "What kind of thesaurus do you use?"

Mark Van Doren answered, "I have no thesaurus. I never use one."

Fred was really impressed. "That sounded to me as if he never consulted a dictionary."

In any case, Fred considered Van Doren's answer to be quite a commentary on his remarkable grasp of the English language.

Fred also recalls, with some amusement, an eating habit of Van Doren's.

"At breakfast Mark would often order hotcakes and when he did, he would first drive a little well down through the middle of the stack, then fill this well with syrup, thus allowing the liquid to permeate the whole stack without running all over the entire plate. He enjoyed explaining his pancake theory."

Eileen thought it very clever and to this day she abides by Mark's plan. Fred, however, frankly admits allegiance to his old hit-or-miss technique, allowing the freely flowing liquid to land where it will — stomach, tablecloth, rug or wallpaper. But whenever pancakes are ordered, the conversation usually turns to Mark and Dorothy Van Doren.

While at the Foundation, the Whitakers came to know Max Eastman, great controversial figure of some years back, and his second wife, Yvette. Over cocktails and coffee dialogue flowed freely.

"Max took a particular shine to Eileen, as do most men. To her he confided that since his revolutionary days his opinions had changed considerably, that the years had mellowed him — stories we both took with a grain of salt. But he was certainly an interesting character with a warm nature. Just before he died a few years ago he wrote Eileen a fascinating letter about his earlier days spent on the Scripps Ranch [of Scripps-Howard newspaper fame] located a few miles from our La Jolla home."

Fred's early hunger to associate with creative minds has been happily appeased throughout his career. He collects friends as avidly as a collector of rare books, Americana, or butterflies, gathers his treasures. Sometimes meetings develop into warm friendships. At other times a chance meeting of hours becomes a memorable occasion.

At a dinner party given by President Ludd Spivey of Florida Southern College at one of New York's plush hotels, Fred had such a meeting with Frank Lloyd Wright.

"We are all familiar with the fact that Wright had a pretty good opinion of himself," Fred commented, "and stories touching on that particular characteristic are numerous, such as the one which tells of his having been a witness in a court case."

Wright was asked by the prosecuting attorney, "What is your name?"

"Frank Lloyd Wright," was the answer.

"What is your profession?"

Wright straightened his tie, threw back his head and replied, "I am the world's greatest architect."

Later, a friend of Wright's said to him, "That was a brash statement you made at the trial. Why did you say such a thing?"

"I had to," Wright replied, "I was under oath."

On the evening of the party alluded to, about twenty guests had been invited. Wright was in his usual form. The table was a long, narrow one, with the host, Spivey, at one end, Wright at the other. Fred was seated on the architect's right hand while Sydney Hollaender, manufacturer of shipping labels and a lover of the arts, was seated at the left.

Wright insisted on poking fun at Hollaender's rotund figure. "I personally thought he was carrying his remarks beyond the point of a joke, but Hollaender took it like a gentleman."

"Finally he said, 'Doctor Wright, I would like you to know that this figure of mine, that you are criticising so freely, was designed by an even greater architect than you.'

"Wright thought for a moment, then waving his finger at Hollaender, replied, 'Well, he may be a greater architect than I, but HE is the only one!'

"I had a long talk with Wright that evening and I remarked that he had apparently been an ardent student of George Bernard Shaw. He admitted that Shaw was one of his idols."

Fred, as we have mentioned before, had been an admirer of the considerable talents of Gordon Grant since his early days of study. Later, they became great friends and he enjoys telling the following anecdote about the famous marine painter:

"He [Grant] lived in New York but spent most of his summers in Gloucester, Massachusetts, where he was a member of the North Shore Arts Association.

"On one occasion he wrote to me in New York saying that the Association was raising funds and requested that I send him a small donation. He was a great wit and always enjoyed a joke, so I sent him a check with the faked declaration that I had sold the letter, with his signature affixed, to an autograph hound for $25 which I was sending along to him, thus doing my day's good deed with no cost to myself.

"I thought this would appeal to his thrifty Scottish nature. But Gordon took the story straight and wrote me saying, 'You're a better man than I am. This is the first time my autograph has been sold for $25.' On numerous occasions he recited this evidence of my sales ability."

Everett Shinn was another famous artist with whom the Whitakers had a fast friendship. Fred remembers him as a "fiery little guy, a most interesting and admirable character."

"Everett Shinn lived on Washington Square in New York City. We lived on Sheridan Square, two blocks away. Eileen and I got to know Everett intimately and frequently we had dinner together at The Athens restaurant on Sixth Avenue and Ninth Street. All of this is in the center of Greenwich Village. The Athens was a meeting place of artists and writers, so we were able to meet quite a few notables there. Yasuo Kuniyoshi was one of the regular patrons.

"We used to spend quite a bit of time in Everett's studio, evenings after dinner. He seemed to be engaged in writing projects most of the time. One of the things he had been working on for several years was a biographical work on each of the members of the Ash Can School. He used to read this material aloud to us.

"Some of it was pretty sensational, such as his version of how George Luks was kicked to death by Negroes in Hell's Kitchen. Everett was a key witness in the inquest into Luks' death. Apparently that story about Luks has never been told. Shortly before his death Everett told us the work was ready for publication. We were never able to learn what happened to his manuscript.

"Shinn admitted to us that he was a great ladies' man. He had been married a number of times and claimed to have built a home for each wife and given it to her after divorce, along with alimony.

"At the time of this conversation, I remember he was seventy-six years old. One day I found him in a rather distraught condition and on my asking what was bothering him he replied, 'You know, it's the same thing that bothers me always — women!' Just before his final illness overtook him he went over with us the plans for a splendid new home which he was preparing to build up the [Hudson] river."

Of course, Fred first came to know Charles Dana Gibson through his published drawings of the *American Girl*. He had been in awe of the freedom with which Gibson executed his pen-and-ink techniques. The artist's Gibson Girl, often shown engaged in outdoor activities, had created a tremendous vogue. The drawings were eventually published in book form.

"I had been an admirer of his work and, as a regular reader of the old humorous magazine *Life*, of which he was president, I had learned quite a bit about his activities.

"In appearance he always reminded me of an English bulldog, though he was really a benign old gentleman.

"After his death I had several luncheon meetings, on art activities, with his widow, one of the famous Langhorne sisters. [The other sister became Lady Astor, M.P. of the British House of Commons.] Actually, I think Mrs. Gibson was the model for the Gibson Girl in her earlier days. The chief thing about her that I recall was her booming voice which could be heard for half a block and which she never bothered to restrain. I remember on one occasion having lunch with her at the Place Pigalle. Whenever she spoke, eyes were directed toward our table from all parts of the restaurant."

The earliest monograph Fred wrote for *American Artist* was on Enrico Monjo, the Spanish sculptor.

"I first heard of Monjo when I was on the Council of the National Academy of Design. A letter had come to the Academy from the government of Spain, telling about the work of their foremost sculptor, Enrico Monjo. They had enclosed a lot of photos of his work and stated that they would like to send an exhibition of the actual sculptures to the United States, and asked if the National Academy of Design would stage it.

"Along with other members of the Council I was very impressed with Monjo's product and I suggested that the Council should give serious consideration to the suggestion. But one member, a sculptor, was extremely critical of his work, which he referred to as a lot of *Barroco Junk,* so the Academy replied we were not in a position to accept the invitation.

"Several years later announcement was made that Monjo's work was on exhibition in New York. It created quite a sensation; even the National Sculpture Society joined in doing Monjo honor.

"Norman Kent, editor of the *American Artist* magazine, asked me to write an article on Monjo. It appeared in the magazine in the May issue of 1957."

Monjo spoke no English but his wife, Josefina, brought along with them from Spain an interpreter named Francisco Coll. The three spent several months in New York. The Whitakers got to know them socially and dined with them a number of times. Monjo also accepted the Whitakers' invitation to visit them in Connecticut.

"On one occasion," Fred recounts, "Eileen and I were dancing a rhumba. When we returned to our table, Francisco Coll said, 'I've seen you two dancing the Rhumba before — in the hotel at Tossa del Mar, on the Costa Brava in Spain.' And sure enough he described the details of our stay in that city, although we had not met there."

"I could write a book on Anna Hyatt Huntington," Fred will assure you with enthusiasm. "She, of course, is the famous sculptress. Her husband, Archer Huntington, was a great philanthropist, the son of Collis B. Huntington, one of the Big Four who built the transcontinental railway. We had been close friends of the family since 1953.

"Archer had been a mighty worker, but after reaching eighty, he looked at life philosophically and, while he continued to give away great sums of money [he once told me he had given away thirty million dollars to a group of interests in the square at 155th and Broadway] he no longer took on new projects.

"In 1969 Anna was ninety-five years of age. We saw her a year before that and she was still active as a sculptor. Seven years ago, just before coming west, I watched her working on the model of a huge equestrian statue. She was standing on a regular carpenter's ladder, about twelve feet above the floor.

"The Huntington home is in West Redding, Connecticut. It is about twenty miles from where we then lived. The estate was enormous, 3,500 acres — or maybe it was 35,000! Whatever its exact size, it had been given to Connecticut as a State Park to be held by Anna during her lifetime.

"Anna used to travel around the estate in a small electric one-seat car with a pistol hanging from her belt, and she knew how to use that pistol, and other firearms, too. On one occasion she told us that with a .22 rifle she had just shot over one hundred squirrels that were literally trying to take over the house.

"From the time we first met the Huntingtons [but not because of it] they never went out on social calls. For one thing, Archer was confined to a wheelchair due to arthritis. Each Sunday afternoon was calling time at the Huntington House — and what callers they were!"

These functions were not attended especially by artists, but by important people in all walks of life, particularly those from Spanish-speaking countries. Among them one might find General Manolo de Villejas, former chief of staff for Francisco Franco of Spain, now in charge of the Army of the Pyrenees; Luis de Urzaiz, Vice President of the Spanish Institute in New York; Enrico Monjo, foremost sculptor of Spain; Laura G. Fraser, American sculptor; Wheeler Williams, American sculptor; Frank Reilly, American painter; John C. Pellew, American painter; and a host of other luminaries and "hero worshippers."

"Archer had a sharp wit and a keen mind and he loved to tilt with anyone who could keep up with him."

Eileen and Fred were the last of the non-family to see Archer alive. He was then eighty-five years old.

"On that last day we found him propped up in bed, sitting against the headboard. He grabbed me, put his arms around me and hugged me like a bear. He was six feet five inches tall and built like a wrestler. Simultaneously he gave me a fervid lecture on what I should do with my so-called talents. He wouldn't be quieted.

"After releasing me he began telling about his journey across Spain on a mule, illustrating some of the points by singing in Arabic, a language he spoke as fluently as he spoke Spanish."

Prior to that time, the Whitakers did not know he had been critically ill. But that day they sensed something was radically wrong. "We decided we'd better leave the bedroom and let him rest. As we reached the door he shouted at us, 'Wait a minute! The next time you see me, I'll be dead'.

"He kept his word. On the following Thursday we attended his funeral."

During the past two decades, watercolor has enjoyed a healthy revival in the United States and Frederic Whitaker has been one of its most enthusiastic champions. Edwin Barrie, director of the Grand Central Galleries in New York City, once called him "Mr. Watercolor." It has become an affectionate nickname, because since 1950 he has devoted himself exclusively to the use of watercolor.

While many artists feel obliged to trick up their aquarelles with gobs of glue, areas of sand, sections of collage, he remains a purist, using watercolor for its own sake, relying on his ability with a brush and the control of his medium.

Not only has he refused to join the mainstream of art which he considers gimmicky, funky or so obscure it must be clarified with a statement, he has little patience with it and when asked for an opinion, minces no words.

"Why does art have to be *explained*?" he asks in a published article. ". . . of what use is a painting if it has to be spelled out? Now, the explainer himself, that is the artist, must have an interpreter. If all this translation is necessary, why not save the trouble of making paintings altogether and simply substitute verbal descriptions of what they ought to mean? Communication is art, art is communication." This is Whitaker's credo.

"He believes in purposeful, careful, and responsible work," said one London reviewer.

So it has always been with this artist who declares in a strong essay on "The Purpose of Painting": "Lack of consideration for the wishes of others leads only to irresponsibility and I see no excuse for artists alone, among workers, claiming the right to be irresponsible . . . expression is wasted unless it also conveys something to the beholder." He includes beauty as necessary to art. To opt for beauty is unique in an age when ugliness is tantamount to a cult. Yet, it is through this unpopular approach that Frederic Whitaker has achieved success.

Much of this success he credits to his knowledge of design. "Throughout my life I have been able to realize the value of having been a designer, an inventor of sorts, and a mechanical draftsman. In these lines one is compelled to calculate and to know how things are done, not in a general way, but down to the finest detail. Such work stimulates one's creative and analytical tendencies.

"Design, in a painting, means the contrived arrangement of masses, colors, values, directions, key, etc., which, added to the chosen theme, makes a perfect picture. No photographic copy of a subject can do that. Pictures, like buildings, airplanes or anything else that serves a purpose, must be designed. And, believe it or not, art must have a purpose beyond that of outlet for the artists' fervor. Design, or lack of it, shows the difference between aesthetic and merely reportorial painting. All art masterpieces have sound design. The rule covers both abstract and representational work. Good abstract examples represent pure design — and that alone can be inspiring and beautiful. As a long time designer [architectural and ecclesiastical metal] I know the importance of pure, non-communicative design. But design alone does not make a picture — unless we change the real meaning of the word. A picture must convey a meaning to the viewer, and this explains my predilection for painting 'realistically' rather than otherwise, for a good picture contains all the qualities of an abstraction in addition to edifying content: atmosphere, depth, meaning and the like. Would I not be dull indeed to throw away deliberately even one of the few faculties given me for making myself understood? That would be like trying to converse without using any words beginning say, with 'S' or 'A'. Such conversation would surely set the speaker apart — which might satisfy some — but we must remember that the real purpose of speech, and art, is not merely to advertise oneself, but to convey thought.

"Well, how do we go about implementing this demand for design in our paintings? Some artists can paint important works with nothing more to follow than a mental plan, developing the details as they proceed, but with my own less retentive mind I like to work out every factor visibly before flooding paint over a full sheet of watercolor paper. It is harder to correct a watercolor application than an oil. With a five-or six-inch sketch, using gouache, I can make repeated changes rapidly, and this I do until the layout and color-and-value relationships leave me unperturbed — for my method is more negative than positive. Usually I can see faults at a glance, though the remedy may escape me for some time.

"The final step in this little pilot painting is to draw the boundaries. This is important. It really means to locate the picture contents within the frame. It is much easier to move the borders to fit the picture material than to move the whole picture across the paper. To make later enlargement possible the proportions of the sketch must be made to correspond with one of my seven stock frame sizes. I must explain that Mrs. Whitaker and I have adopted stock sizes that we both follow. Thus we can order especially made frames in numbers and have no difficulty in shifting pictures from one to another.

"With all problems worked out in the small sketch I can then paint my large finished picture, in transparent color only, confidently and without fumbling, assured of good design and, I hope, with a directness that at least gives an *appearance* of spontaneity."

Fred is never shy in expressing his ideas about the importance of art that is meaningful. Artist and critic alike have always been aware of this, including the writer-publisher Peyton Boswell, guiding spirit behind the *Art Digest* for many years, a magazine founded by his father. He was the friend of noted artists and did much to influence art during his lifetime. In an evaluation of Fred's paintings made years ago, his words ring true today: "His [Whitaker's] mind is definitely set on the meaning and purpose of art. Despite the interminable discussions, he insists the issue is clear. For him, art has one prime purpose — to add to the world's store of beauty."

Fred is also among the first to give credit where credit is due, and the procedural experience he acquired in the Masonic Order, he credits as having been important and beneficial to his later progress.

When referring to benefits Fred is not speaking alone of those gained from the formal teaching of Masonry in regard to good fellowship but also to the system used by the Masonic Order, arranged in graduated steps, which one must take to achieve their high degrees.

"I was 'in line' in the Council in 1926 and as is commonly known, all Masonic ritual and lectures are prescribed and must be said from memory." Consider Fred's shyness, that bogey-boo that had plagued him from childhood! To face an audience of even two people, let alone speak from memory, was a very large order. "With my ingrained reticence," Fred admitted, "I feel sure this was the only system that could ever have gotten me on my feet."

The steps in Masonry, then, coupled with what he had learned from compulsory dictation, gave him the self-assurance he now possesses, although he claims that any such assurance is only a fraction of what it appears to be. But it does account for "whatever favors and advancements have been conferred upon me in art and other non-business ventures."

In 1916 Fred was made a Master Mason. Within a brief number of years, after passing through all the intervening Masonic bodies, including the Knights Templar or Commandry, he was accepted in the Consistory or 3rd Degree Division. He also looks upon this experience as an apprenticeship of sorts and likes to compare the steps in Masonry to the apprenticeship offered by the old masters, to anyone who wished to become an artist.

"Often I think of these lessons when discussing current art thought. Under the prescription of our present day art establishment that controls art education in virtually all our schools and colleges, the student must never be allowed to copy anything, the only purpose of teaching being to develop the student's own imagination and uncover his particular personality.

"Inasmuch as progress in any field always comes by gradual development with each step springing from the one that went before, the truth, of course, is that the best art work the world has produced has come from the apprentice system, where the novice first copied and copied from the works of his master and other professionals until he was able to find a school or trend of his own — to mix his own ideas with those imposed upon him.

"Despite the aims of the present day taste-makers and their prescription of copying, the fact remains that at no other time have so many artists copied from so many others. In this present period of supposed originality, where theoretically there should be as many styles of paintings as there are artists, the work of all avant-garde artists can be easily grouped into a very limited number of mannerism categories.

"There are those who can learn only by copying, at least in the early stages, and I must confess to being a member of that group. I am satisfied that nearly everyone else belongs there. And what I have to say about art practice applies with equal truth to virtually every other skill, science or activity. The lessons of Masonry have opened many doors for me."

Masonry, then, was a stepping stone to the adventures ahead in the complex world of art and business. His experiences as a professional artist really began in 1941. His initial contact with art groups, however, came about when he joined the Providence Watercolor Club in 1924 and the Providence Art Club in 1926. The Providence Watercolor Club immediately elected him president.

When he arrived in New York his reputation as a designer preceded him. He was owner of a successful business with branches in New York and Chicago. His rapid strides as a watercolorist were already attracting attention.

Generally speaking, artists are not clever in business, they lack organization, have hang-ups about balancing a budget, know little or nothing about effective selling. No one is quicker to recognize the unique combination of good artist and good businessman than another artist. Small wonder he was invited to join all the art associations of any consequence and to be elected to a number of them.

"I'm just a man who can't say NO!" Fred will tell you. The truth of the matter is, and he will deny it, the man is a born executive.

It wasn't as though he needed additional activity at this time. World War II was creating complications in the manufacturing business; one was the shortage of manpower. Nevertheless, his ability to organize, dispatch work effectively, and get things done in short order, made his presence in any organization a great asset.

The Allied Artists of America (1942 to 1966), the American Watercolor Society (since 1938), the Fine Arts Federation of New York (Director from 1947 to 1950), and the Salmagundi Club (since 1941) are some of the organizations to which Whitaker has lent his talents and seemingly endless vitality.

The Salmagundi Club, oldest art club in the country, was founded in 1870. During its first seventy years, its roster of members included virtually all the illustrious artists in the United States: Abbey, La Farge, Chase, Innes, Murphy, Pyle, Ranger, Tiffany, Zorn, Biggs among them.

Fred recounts some of his thoughts on fellow member Walter Biggs with affection:

"We met and ate together frequently at the Club. Biggs was a great artist and a great illustrator. I knew him from 1941 until 1966 when he returned to Salem, Virginia, his birthplace. He died there in 1968. He often told me of his early days when he was a pal of Strangler Lewis, wrestling champion of the world, in the twenties.

"Walter was noted for his organized untidiness. Be that as it may, he certainly got results. I remember that in one corner of the room was a stack of books and magazines about four feet high and about the same width on the floor. The books were just thrown into a heap. This was part of his reference material.

"He worked in a similarly sloppy fashion. Doing a watercolor he would paint with his paper vertical, on an easel. Naturally, as he applied the liquid color with the brush in his right hand, the color would run down the paper. But he was ready for it! With a sponge in his left hand he would catch it. The two hands appeared to be equally busy. Walter would have a worried expression on his face, as though he felt he could never finish the job. But he did — always with a nice, juicy picture."

At the time Fred became a member of the Salmagundi Club, it was an "unofficial prep school" for the National Academy of Design, at least in the department of painting.

In fact, one long table was called the Academician's Table and anyone lacking Academy membership would never presume to sit at it without an invitation from the elect. It was Walter Biggs who proposed Fred for membership in the National Academy of Design. In 1945 he was elected an Associate; several years later he was made an Academician.

On three separate occasions he declined invitations by the nominating committee to stand as candidate for the presidency. His usual candor colored his declining the honor: "It would have been impossible to carry out the reforms or developments that the Academy needs."

The touchy situation between the two factions, representative and avant-garde painters, seemed irreconcilable. But hope for making changes at least caused Fred to join a group headed by Wheeler Williams, sculptor, to attempt making reforms. The trouble, however, appeared to be deeper than just that of painting. It was largely concerned with politics and ideologies.

The warm friendships made with members outweighed the frustrations. One of these friendships was with Dean Cornwell, celebrated American muralist of whom Fred says:

"Most of the time between 1953 and 1963, I was a member of the National Academy Council (Board of Directors). So was Dean Cornwell. At the meetings it was customary for the members to take the same seats each time, so I sat next to Dean. On meeting days we had plenty of time for discussions. In that way I learned a lot about his former activities, especially about his working with Frank Brangwyn, famous English artist. Dean was an extremely modest person, for all his acclaim."

It may seem incredible to those unacquainted with the history of the American Watercolor Society, to realize it was founded right after the close of the Civil War. Its early roster of members included practically every artist of prominence of that era.

Through the years, however, the society's management had become ingrown. Because the large majority had little voice in its affairs, they had little interest in its activities, except to participate in the annual exhibition. Then the best watercolors the country had to offer were put on display.

In 1940 when Fred was elected president, the Society was still being run in a sketchy manner, with many details left to two persons: the artist Harry de Maine, and his wife, one of Alfred A. Knopf publishing company's most able readers, who dedicated her spare time to an overwhelming labor of love.

Fred's job as president was to distribute the work among a greater number of members. "It was incumbent on me to keep all workers busy." Within a couple of years membership mushroomed, several hundred of well-informed members could be depended on in almost any emergency. Board meetings were held regularly, general meetings were scheduled semi-annually.

Fred was retained as president for seven years. Of that active period he declared: "If those years accomplished anything . . . one contribution was in showing members the importance of their own organization and encouraging pride in their membership."

Today the American Watercolor Society's exhibits are recognized as the most important of their kind anywhere in the world. As a member, director, or president over a period of thirty-three years, Fred came to know virtually all the outstanding artists in the country who work in watercolor. Among them was Andrew Wyeth who "even as a boy was a remarkably fine artist. But his meteoric rise to fame has taken place within a relatively few years. Twenty years ago his watercolors could have been purchased at the A.W.S. exhibitions for $500. Prices today are, of course, way up in the thousands. On two occasions at my request, Andy gave painting demonstrations before the society members and gallery visitors at the galleries of the National Academy of New York."

Mike Engel was responsible for bringing about Fred's first one-man show in New York at the Ferargil Galleries and for helping to launch him in "the New York art mill."

Engel was an odd sort of genius in the field of publicity. As director of promotion for M. Grumbacher, Inc., manufacturer of artist's materials, his job was to call on leading artists throughout the country and offer them batches of Grumbacher propaganda in the form of paints, brushes and the like. His powers of persuasion were sufficient to get them involved in all kinds of promotional projects.

Ben Messick and his wife Velma, Long Beach artists who traveled with Engel on a demonstration tour, were astounded at the man's energy. "He kept up a barrage of correspondence that would have exhausted the average person." Ben recalls. "Artists were kept in constant touch with his activities, if only by a few words on a postcard. He never overlooked an opportunity to advance the success of Grumbacher. No one could doubt his sincerity. No one has done so much for the American artist."

Engel had the unique talents of an old-fashioned medicine man. He was aggressive, amusing, full of ideas, and these ideas were to a large extent responsible for the rapid growth of the Grumbacher concern in the past thirty years. His weather eye was always casting about for new talent. One day in 1933 he called at Fred's office in Providence, introduced himself, and asked for his participation in a traveling exhibit of watercolor paintings.

Here and there Engel would establish small art societies and ply members with art materials. One of them was called The Audubon Artist's Group, so named because its first meeting was held in a building on the old farm of John James Audubon, located in the present Audubon section of New York City near the George Washington Bridge. It was before this group that Fred, as a gesture to Engel, gave several lectures and demonstrations of his techniques. But Fred didn't consider the group to have any real standing; he repeatedly refused Engel's entreaties that he become its president. Fred was already president of several regional organizations. He continued to run the Foley and Dugan Company which sold Catholic religious articles to priests and nuns across the country. Simultaneously he ran the G. H. Seffert Company which manufactured and imported religious articles and sold them wholesale to the religious stores in the larger cities of the United States. The plant in New York employed fifty people.

But Engel was not one to give up easily. Finally, in 1943, needled by Engel's badgering, Fred suggested a counterplan.

"I'll tell you what I'll do. If you want to have a first-rate national art society organized, I'll do it. Bring in those you want for key positions and we'll go to work."

A list of 450 painters and sculptors from throughout the United States, "the cream of the crop," was made, from which members were to be drawn. It was decided that members would be accepted by invitation only.

For the purpose of prestige it was agreed to have a large Board of Directors, comprised of the country's best and most representative artists from all schools of art.

It is doubtful that any other national art society has ever been organized in such record time. With the help of his office secretary, Fred plunged into the business of distributing invitations and informative material. The twenty-five topflight artists promptly accepted their positions as members of the Board.

A letterhead mentioning these important names was printed and on these letterheads they addressed membership invitations to the 450. Four hundred accepted immediately. Within months after starting from scratch, Audubon Artists, Inc. was an operating organization whose total membership represented probably the largest gathering of artistic talent ever assembled at one time in this country.

Because Fred maintained a business office, a secretary, and the necessary equipment for such a job, he not only assumed the task of organization, but good-naturedly assumed most of the initial expense. Few, if any, of the members realized the large financial outlay entailed in bringing about such satisfactory results in such a short time.

It was through membership in Artists For Victory that Fred had his first close look at subversive activities. The objective for Artists For Victory was laudible but it was promptly infiltrated by Communists who began their usual machinations within the art field.

From repeated encounters with these machinations Fred also learned that "the real danger of Communism lies not so much in the Communists themselves but in the soft-headed Americans, who, in their anxiety to be fair, allow themselves to become potent allies of the cause."

Goodwill among nations, it has often been said, would be accelerated, strengthened, and made to work through the arts. Attempts by various groups to bring about such a harmonious state have been made, but seldom with any lasting effect.

Under the aegis of UNESCO, the International Association of Plastic Arts was set up in Paris about 1952, for the purpose of bringing together the workers in the visual arts throughout the world. Each nation was to have its own committee, and representatives of these committees were scheduled to convene every two or three years at a city previously agreed upon.

As president of the American Watercolor Society, Fred was invited to attend when the American Committee was formed. Lawrence Grant White, President of the National Academy of Design, appointed him official delegate from N.A.D. to I.A.P.A.

Fred tells something of the nature of this association in his direct manner:

"At a later organizational meeting Cecil Howard was elected President; I was made First Vice-President; and Harold Weston, Second Vice-President. As First Vice-President I was called upon to preside at a number of meetings. In I.A.P.A. I saw a perfect example of the manner in which a pressure organization is set up and how power can be wielded and influence built by a very small group of individuals, when working in the name of a presumably widespread organization.

"The American Committee was run by 'The Boys', and undoubtedly still is, for, while a rightist organization may turn left, a leftist society can never become conservative, because of the simple, natural law that the bland host, no matter how large, must eventually be overcome by the agent of fermentation within it, no matter how small."

Fred was the only conservative director and it didn't take him long to see why he had been chosen. "It was because of the standard left-wing practice of including one or two rightists in their deliberate groups to give the impression of all-inclusiveness. Pointing out that I, Vice-President of the National Academy, the oldest and foremost art society of America, was also First Vice-President of the I.A.P.A., gave the latter great propaganda material, of which it took definite advantage."

After a short period of observing at close range how the selection of jury members, nominating committee members, national and international delegation members were dictatorially appointed, how decisions were made in line with the party desires, and how all opposing views were politely but firmly squelched, Fred asked Academy President Lawrence White to allow him to resign from the I.A.P.A. office.

White, however, felt it was advantageous to maintain a listening post within I.A.P.A. and asked that Fred continue.

"The listening post idea was a good one, of course," Fred pointed out, "but in my opinion its value was more than offset by the disadvantage of allowing I.A.P.A. to go about the country, and the world, claiming it represented the thinking of the National Academy."

Several years later, Fred again proposed separating from the group. John Harbeson, then Incumbent Academy President, called a special meeting of the Council, to which Henry Billings and I.A.P.A. President Leon Kroll, were invited. Fred was asked to repeat his charges. In brief, they were: "1. I.A.P.A. claimed that it represented the art fraternity of the United States whereas it actually represented the opinions of very few more than a half dozen individuals; 2. In spite of his continued exhortations, the I.A.P.A. Board had refused to expand the field of representation or to allow art societies outside the New York City district to have any representation whatever; 3. Monthly meetings accomplished nothing other than to approve decisions already made by the inner circle and these were all slanted in one direction."

Fred said that "Billings and Kroll replied by quoting the Constitution which, theoretically, made provisions for fair and general representation, but the practical considerations were such that fulfillment was impossible. So far as I know, no extra New York organizations have been granted representation to this day."

Later, the Academy Council voted for continued membership in I.A.P.A. President Harbeson accepted Fred's resignation to that body and appointed Edmondo Quattrocchi to replace him.

But Quattrocchi also became disillusioned with I.A.P.A. and within the next couple of years denounced I.A.P.A. before the Academy Council in more explosive terms than Fred had.

It was at that time that the Council voted to sever its connections with the I.A.P.A. Since that time a number of national art group members have also resigned.

Whitaker held other directorships: in the National Society of Painters in Casein, The Fine Arts Federation of New York, the Municipal Arts Society, and the National Arts Club, plus association with art societies across the country and in England. All this participation gave him a better than usual insight into the mechanics of the art business in general.

Andrew Carnegie once remarked: "The average person puts in twenty-five percent of his energy and ability into his work. The world takes off its hat to those who put in more than fifty percent of their capacity, and stands on its head for those few and far between souls who devote one hundred percent."

In that case we must stand on our heads to Frederic Whitaker.

Fred was told repeatedly as a child that NOTHING should be wasted. The advice was not wasted on Fred.

From the time he obtained his first designing job — that wonderful period of discovery when, after putting in a full day's work, he spent half the night studying, haunting libraries, taking correspondence courses — until he married, he was establishing a pattern. It is a pattern that is still evident in his daily activities.

Prolific though Fred has been as an artist, that record has been matched by his career as a writer. Because of greater exposure, a writer usually acquires a larger audience than an artist. If, like Frederic Whitaker, his name appears frequently in print through the years, it may encourage a deluge of mail.

There are the invitations to lecture, to write books, to jury shows, and to teach. These are some of the fringe benefits accorded a writer. There are also quite a number of requests from novices who wish to become authors. "How did you start writing?" they ask him. "How did you learn to write?"

Fred answers succinctly, in words like these: "What little I know about writing comes from two sources: dictating letters and from a Sherwin Cody correspondence course in English to which I subscribed when office work was first thrust on me.

"I doubt that any other artist has been guilty of so many involvements, and I am sure that I have sat on more art juries than any other American painter. The information thus acquired helps me immeasurably in my writing of articles."

When an artist, Fred claims, is found who can state his case verbally, even reasonably well, he is put to work as a writer and lecturer.

"I was first invited by Ralph Fabri to write short treatises on art subjects for *Today's Art*, a periodical that is distributed by art supply stores without charge to their customers."

That was followed by other invitations to write for publications dealing with art.

The Artist, of London, asked him to do a number of instructional articles. He was also offered a space in each month's issue to be called the "Frederic Whitaker Page" in which he might philosophize at will.

But what most influenced Fred's writing career was his acquaintance with Ernest Watson. It solidified his writing in the direction of *art*. Certainly no account of Fred Whitaker's life would be complete without inclusion of the famous writer, artist, and publisher and the magazine which brought the two of them so closely together. For Fred it marked the beginning of a long association with *American Artist,* of which Watson was one of the founders, and cemented a long and rewarding friendship between the two men.

In 1918 Watson and Arthur Guptill, a fellow teacher at the Pratt Institute in Brooklyn, joined forces and founded a magazine which they called *Pencil Points*. It was a normal outgrowth of mutual interests since both of these men were consummate draftsmen.

Architectural renderings and pencil drawings were the magazine's main features. It remained in circulation until around 1930 when it evolved into *American Artist,* a slick monthly devoted to art and artists in the United States and their techniques.

The art student was Guptill's particular enthusiasm, and it was at his insistence that the newly formed monthly set aside a few pages of each issue for the amateur, to be written and edited by Guptill himself.

In the early fifties Guptill became ill and believing the illness would be of short duration, he summoned Fred to ghostwrite his pages. This Fred agreed to do, under Guptill's name. It was his introduction as a regular writer for *American Artist*.

"This work for the beginners had no particular appeal for me. I have always been more interested in the thought behind art production than in its technical aspects. But I did learn a great deal more than many of my readers, especially from my association with these two great teachers and publishers."

When it was realized that Guptill would not recover, the Amateur Pages were run under Whitaker's name; when Guptill died, they were discontinued. Everyone on the staff had opposed them, anyway. Watson, now being senior editor, prevailed upon Fred to write occasional articles on various artists. During this period he also worked with Norman Kent, a gifted writer and artist who later became editor of the magazine. Fred had met him years before through various art societies. At that time Kent was writing articles for it.

Ernest Watson was a colorful man, completely individual, who left his mark on anyone privileged to work with him. The fame of his unorthodox attire was secondary only to his skills as writer, artist, and friend to countless struggling creative people.

Tall and gaunt, his irregular features in a ruddy complexioned New England face seemed to glow with a spark from within. After taking a trip out west, his costumes became more Bohemian. He would not hesitate to enter one of his favorite New York lunchtime haunts in a western hat, an ankle-length plaid cape with yellow plaid lining, a blue western shirt, and a flowing black artist's tie. Often he wore a beret. This odd mix-match of clothing seemed perfectly agreeable on him, perhaps because he wore them without a trace of self-consciousness and with a natural grace.

It was this unusual, original man then who helped build greater confidence in Fred as a writer. "I naturally felt flattered when he sought me out and took notice of me in a literary way."

When Ernest Watson disposed of his holdings in the Watson–Guptill Corporation in 1956 to Guptill's son, Leighton, Norman Kent became editor-in-chief. He had served as an art editor for *Reader's Digest* and *True*. Thus began a closer association between Whitaker and the articulate Kent.

Doing such a number of articles on well-known artists, plus occasional editorials or "philosophical outbursts," Whitaker was able to gain a comprehensive view of art life in America and to become personally acquainted with a very large portion of the exhibiting artists in the United States.

Today half of Fred's time is spent writing. Most artists worthy of the name make good copy. To varying degrees they are stimulating, interesting, fascinating — although all are not articulate with words (that, of course, should be the writer's job). But once in a while a writer is handed a real plum. That is how Fred felt when he unexpectedly found himself writing "A Day with Disney."

Fred's admiration for Walt Disney dated back to thirty years before the article when, in front of the Providence Art Club, he loudly proclaimed Disney as *"the contemporary artist who had contributed most to the advancement of the visual arts."*

Amid shouts of laughter from other members Fred reminded them that the real greats in art are so-called because they have brought a new quality to the art of painting. "Da Vinci, for instance, showed us the possibilities of Chiaroscuro; Rembrandt, among other achievements, brought Chiaroscuro to its finest flower; Turner showed us how to paint light, and so on."

To the scoffers he emphasized that Disney's contribution — animation — was an entirely new factor, probably "more revolutionary than that effected by any other single artist, and the artistic quality of the first efforts, or their lack, had no bearing upon the potential value . . . the full possibilities could not be known for many years, and the inventors themselves might later be amazed by the magnitude of the developments. Let us remember the examples of the Wright Brothers, Marconi, Doctor Banting and others of their breed."

The thoughts in the foregoing statements tell us a great deal about Fred's approach to art in general. Having dealt from childhood with art's practical and aesthetic nature he fully realizes the value of both.

Art and philosophy remain Fred's favorite subjects in writing, the one often hingeing on or overlapping the other. Numerous essays have been written. To clarify an idea, he says he *must* get it down on paper. This is what he calls one of his *random reflections* on matters artistic entitled "Art and the Public."

ART AND THE PUBLIC

There are those who like to infer that art — painting and sculpture — is a hallowed subject to be discussed intelligently only by those especially educated. This means that the general public should refrain from judging and should look up to its betters for opinions.

This is a modern conception, for in all earlier ages art was contrived to convey messages directly. The artist was the great explainer. With pictures and sculpture he illustrated important truths to help the humble and erudite alike. So it seems odd, as under today's curious outlook, that anyone might suggest that the artist needs an interpreter.

A professional story-teller can describe an incident in a concise and entertaining or edifying manner, where one less skilled would be dull. Both subject matter and style of presentation are required for a successful story. A brilliant discourse on a trivial thought can have no lasting value. The superior manner of telling, plus the choice of a worthwhile subject, constitutes art. And so it is with picture making — exactly.

The non-artist is likely to judge art too much upon the score of subject matter or theme, but he should remember that subjects other than pretty can be important also. Art need not always be pleasant, but it should say *something* and say it in an understandable manner.

In contrast to our opening premise, many will contend that the artistic taste of Mr. John Citizen functions on a higher plane than does that of the professional interpreter. Well, the public may be misled by tawdry subjects at times, but nearly always it will admire really fine paintings, without knowing why. In any case, no form of art can have enduring success unless it appeals to the generality of people. For some time certain followers of peculiar "isms" have dominated the stage, but they haven't satisfied the people. That accounts for the confusion in art today.

It will be a great day when the non-artist sheds his awe of the museum and asserts his God-given right to express himself on what he sees on its walls.

In 1954 Ernest Watson was acting as a consultant and a book editor for the Reinhold Publishing Company, and it was at this time that he asked Fred to write *Whitaker on Watercolor*, a book on watercolor instruction.

"The most acceptable instructions are those which begin with 'This is what you have to do'. Then people can see what is required of them and there is nothing difficult or complicated about it."

With these thoughts in mind, Fred began to draft his book. Eleven months later, *Whitaker on Watercolor* appeared on the bookstands. Covering the subject from its fundamentals through pictorial planning and advanced art thought, it became and still remains a popular and definitive book in its field.

Whitaker on Watercolor was followed by *Guide to Painting Better Pictures*. Other publications in which Whitaker's work has been featured are: *Watercolor Demonstrated* by Ernest W. Watson and Norman Kent (Watson–Guptill, 1945); *Watercolor Methods* by Norman Kent (Watson–Guptill, 1945); *100 Watercolor Techniques* by Norman Kent (Watson–Guptill, 1968); *History of the American Watercolor Society* by Ralph Fabri (Quinn Company Publishers, 1968); *Twenty-Four Watercolorists* by Norman Kent (as yet unreleased). His work has also been the subject of numerous articles in a variety of publications.

During World War II and its shortage of male help, Fred again found himself in charge of both the Providence and the New York plant. After the war it was decided that his son and son-in-law (who had both worked in the plant) would now take over the business. When arrangements were satisfactorily completed, Fred was free at last to do nothing but paint.

Around the first part of January 1950, Fred and Eileen retired from business to devote their lives to companionship, to paint the way they wanted to paint, and to live in an artistic environment among others interested in the arts. A trip to the west coast convinced them they could be happily transplanted from Norwalk, Connecticut to La Jolla, California.

After twenty-two years the Whitakers' marriage is still alive and vital. It is frequently said that no house is large enough for two artists. The Whitakers have disproved this and both careers have prospered. The roof under which they spend most of their time protects a sprawling, casual, charming house located high on a hill overlooking La Jolla and its beautiful bay on the Pacific Ocean.

They work together in one spacious studio that is arranged in a way that neither one cramps the other's style. Eileen works slowly, she claims, agonizing over every watercolor. The ecstasy, i.e., the result, is well worth the bittersweet agony, if that is what it may be called.

Fred, through years of painting and experimenting, has become extremely facile. He is a sound disciplinarian, knows exactly what he wants. He approaches his work from both the aesthetic and the practical angle. This enables him to work rapidly and with assurance. To him painting is a source of deep enjoyment.

"Women nearly always like my paintings best," Eileen explains. "Men like Fred's work. A sale may be lost for one of Fred's watercolors because the wife insists on buying one of mine. Or vice versa."

The Whitakers find this amusing. "It has often been suggested that we have separate one-man shows. Fred and I don't wish to do that. What difference does it make? It's all in the family."

Eileen, who may sign her paintings either Eileen Monaghan or Eileen Monaghan Whitaker, is one of only three women artists ever to be elected an Associate of the National Academy in the watercolor division. Her work is in great demand and has found its way into many first-rate collections.

Travel has kept the Whitakers' subject matter fresh and in a constant state of flux. They returned from several lengthy trips to Europe with bulging notebooks and numerous photographs for reference which are still being used as source material.

Since anchoring their roots in California soil, they have interspersed concentrated periods of painting in their studio with short trips up and down the coast and to various sections of the Southwest — far less frequently to the East.

One of the Whitakers' favorite locations is Mexico. Together they have explored many parts of this colorful country.

At eighty, Frederic Whitaker is hale and hearty; he appears to be much younger. There is a bounce to his step, a twinkle in his eye. His creative output equals and excels that of many artists half his age. He has the enthusiasm of a young man about to embark on a new adventure.

"For many years I have lived in a state of contentment," he will tell you, "but this was not always so."

Certainly not in his childhoood, as we have already learned. This was often bleak, sometimes bordering on the sordid. "According to the rules propounded by the psychiatric fraternity, I should have been, justifiably, a criminal, a dope addict, an alcoholic or a psychotic. I am none of these."

Being always productive is to his credit. It has kept him interested and lively.

"I am always a bit disturbed when I read of projects being arranged by do-gooders for the senior citizens to fill in the time they themselves presumably do not know how to occupy. Had these citizens acquired a life purpose earlier they wouldn't be able to find *enough time* for their needs, and they would have great fun and, possibly, profit in pursuing it."

In a general way, the great aim of life is to achieve happiness, with happiness meaning many things to many people. "To some," Fred points out, "it is the accumulation of riches; to others, it is power. Political power, for instance. To bask in the adulation of the public means much to a great number.

"But I imagine, to the average person, happiness connotes a condition in which he is called upon to do nothing, where he has the means to procure whatever he desires and where most of his time will be taken up with such diversions as travel, entertainment, games, and that which is usually referred to as worldly pleasure.

"With the exception of the last named, all imply work of a kind, for one can seldom achieve much in any line without effort. But to be essentially happy, we must have a goal or purpose. If we really believe in that purpose, all effort expended in its fulfillment becomes pleasure. A goal, however, should be a worthy one, carefully chosen, for the gratification of ego alone is likely to become bitter in the end."

A reader might suggest that Fred Whitaker's life, according to his own statements, has been a haphazard one, a series of assignments thrust upon him. Could it be that he himself had no purpose in life?

But Fred stands his ground: "It is true that I have followed no schedule or timetable of purpose. My overall policy has been simply to handle each job given me, to the best of my ability, in spite of my limitations."

This attitude has always opened new doors for him. "In analyzing my own activities, I realize now that actually I did have several purposes, kept alive by nondetailed thoughts in mental storage."

Most of us are aware that our goals change throughout our lifetime. Brought up in a household in which cash was paid for everything, Whitaker learned to appreciate the value of money. To accumulate wealth, however, has never been his goal; in fact, he tends to be overgenerous. It is his hope that, probably through his paintings, he can leave a little to posterity.

In this thought Fred has been encouraged by the Art Center of Syracuse University. In 1965 he wrote his autobiography. Doctors Martin H. Bush, Frank P. Piskor, and Lawrence Schmeckabier have established a Frederic Whitaker Manuscript Collection in memory of his achievements. This includes records, correspondence, working sketches, drawings, paintings, photographs, notes, exhibition catalogs, clippings, fan mail, manuscripts of books, essays and articles — i.e., a home for everything related to Frederic Whitaker, permanently arranged for historians, artists, and students.

Fred's autobiography "I Marched in the Parade" was written as the result of a conversation with Dr. Martin H. Bush. Dr. Bush is in charge of the Frederic Whitaker Documentary File of Syracuse University.

Throughout his long career Frederic Whitaker has received numerous citations, honors and awards — over one hundred and fifty major awards for watercolor paintings in national and regional competitive exhibitions.

Whitaker is represented by work in many private collections and over thirty museums, including the Metropolitan Museum of Art, National Academy of Design, Hispanic Museum, and the I.B.M. Collection in New York City, as well as museums in Abilene (Texas), Syracuse (New York), Albion (Michigan), Lakeland (Florida), Frye Museum (Seattle, Washington), and the Museum of Fine Art (Boston).

Whitaker sums up his life by saying: "I can't claim to have been the 'master of my fate' and the 'captain of my soul' but my course has been simply that of perceiving openings and developing them. I have engaged in a great many kinds of work and enjoyed them all as long as they were productive. Painting in watercolor has been, so far, my favorite work. Had I to do it all over again, my route would be more direct, though I am sure my eventual goal would be, as it is today, that of a painter."

THE WATERCOLORS

A TOUR OF THE RUINS

Watercolor, 24 x 22 inches, 1970

Cuenca, Spain, halfway between Madrid
and Valencia, is the site of these weather-beaten structures.
To add life to the ancient architecture, the artist
added two groups of figures, using them for interest
as well as contrast to the mellowed yellow and pink tones
of the walls and to denote scale.

FREDERIC WHITAKER, N.A.

BIRD WATCHERS

Watercolor, 29 x 21 inches, 1969

This is a good example of the manner of making
an interesting painting from an essentially black subject.
James McNeil Whistler was once challenged to do this.
He produced a masterful composition by painting a man in
formal black attire, but in order to make it attractive
he showed the gentleman holding a lady's colorful shawl as
he awaited her. The basis of this painting is Mexican
women dressed in black. Black will harmonize with any color
and this painting has been made appealing by the
introduction of a purely contrived, moderately colorful setting.
The women, when seen by the artist, were standing in a
sidewalk market surrounded by pottery of all shapes and sizes.

MURKY RIVER

Watercolor, 21 x 29 inches, 1968

The artist and his wife Eileen crossed over this
ancient Roman bridge as they were motoring from Madrid
to Caceras. To recall the exact form and detail at such
time as he might need it, black and white
photographs were made on the spot. To break the monotony
of "just another painting of a bridge," Whitaker
added the small figures and cart. "People always like
signs of life in a picture," he says.

Springville (Utah) Art Association, 1970, Best in Show, $1000

FACADE

Watercolor, 30 x 22 inches, 1971

"Fascinated by a particularly fine church doorway
in San Miguel de Allende, Mexico, I made an accurate, detailed,
black and white photo of the doorway itself.
Using the doorway as a base and improvising
different surrounding details, I have made four different
paintings of the subject."

DUSTY TRAIL

Watercolor, 21 x 29 inches, 1966

In juxtaposition to the horizontal arrangement
of cattle and figures in the foreground, the artist introduces
an area of tall "pipe organ" cactus in fresh green
washes of color, giving the picture drama, contrast, form,
and color. The rich dark greens behind the cacti
weave in and out, the great clouds of dust project
the cattle forward. This is a composite of fact and fancy,
something seen and something imagined.

Courtesy of Blair Galleries, Ltd., Santa Fe, New Mexico

THIS PIG GOES TO MARKET

Watercolor, 30 x 22 inches, 1970

When you ask people to pose, you never get
what you want, the artist claims. Without the boy's seeing him,
Whitaker photographed him. In the painting he placed
the pig in a box with the boy's figure at an angle
to accommodate the weight of the animal. Imagination
provided the other details.

HOUSES ON A HILLSIDE

Watercolor, 21 x 29 inches, 1958

When the Whitakers first discovered Gerona, a hillside
town north of Barcelona, they had not realized it was a favorite
painting and sketching spot of many artists. Drawings
were made from various angles. Later when Whitaker
painted the subject in his studio, he found it so intriguing that
he painted the landscape from several angles.

Collection of Mr. and Mrs. Edwin S. Larsen, La Jolla, California

New Haven Paint and Clay Club, 1958
Jordan Marsh Exhibition, Boston, 1958
Washington, D.C. Watercolor Society, 1960
American Artists Professional League, New York, 1963

TOLEDO BRIDGE

Watercolor, 25 x 22 inches, 1965

The artist saw this handsome old bridge as he was driving to Toledo, Spain. "Spanish baroque architecture and ornament — one step above rococo — lends itself to watercolor," he points out. "What might be considered vulgar from a designer's viewpoint, may be beautiful as a painting."

ANTICIPATING THE CEREMONY

Watercolor, 22 x 27 inches, 1970

In the Laguna Pueblo in southwest New Mexico
preparations were being made for the annual ceremony the
next day. The entire landscape and buildings of
gray-brown monotone are typical of certain parts
of that country. The Indians in their brightly colored clothing
supply the relief and contrast that such a subject demands.

FREE LUNCH

Watercolor, 29 x 21 inches, 1969

This is pure fantasy, a swirling pattern
of giant bees dining on some of their favorite blossoms.
In his research the artist made innumerable sketches
of bees, studying the detail on a dead bee under a strong
microscope, rearranging his composition until
he arrived at the one seen in this watercolor.

Collection of Charles and Emma Frye Art Museum, Seattle, Washington

FREDERIC WHITAKER, N.A.

THE PATIENT ONE

Watercolor, 22 x 27 ½ inches, 1969

"The thing that attracted me in this scene in Spain
was the small boy with the large load. Later when I composed
the picture I started simply by drawing the donkey with
his load in small scale. Then I painted a background that was
imaginative and placed the boy to balance the composition."

FREDERIC WHITAKER N.A.

POULTRY MERCHANT

Watercolor, 29 x 21 inches, 1967

The artist quietly watched this colorful poultry
merchant. Adding imaginary but typical background this
award-winning watercolor was produced.
Whitaker displays his virtuosity here with the tricky medium,
notably in the way he has used the white of the paper
in the man's costume, as a dominant form.
He ties the painting together with rich yet neutral tones
and accents of brilliant red.

Collection of Mr. Richard Dyson, La Mesa, California

National Arts Club, 1968, First Award for Watercolor

TREE SHADOWS

Watercolor, 25 x 22 inches, 1971

This is an interpretation of a doorway in Oaxaca, Mexico.
"On the spot I decided what the composition should embrace.
Then I made a pencil sketch to fix that composition.
Next came a snapshot to show the exact detail of the door.
In the studio, months later, I worked out a
compositional design, in color, from the various notes, and
then enlarged the whole to its finished size."

FREDERIC WHITAKER, N.A.

ON THE ROCKS

Watercolor, 14 x 20 inches, 1965

The locale is Lanesville, Massachusetts, on Cape Ann.
This is a straight landscape painting which is fairly realistic.
The small boat was added to the foreground
but otherwise the artist painted what he saw. The artist
has also achieved a mood of peacefulness and contentment
that adds greatly to the charm of the picture.

BOVINE HANGOUT

Watercolor, 30 x 21 inches, 1968

Artists seem fascinated with windmills; this fascination
extends to those who buy paintings. Whitaker has captured
a romantic mood with windmill, silo, and cattle,
seen as the Whitakers travelled by car through Arizona.
The sky, painted spontaneously with a bold brush, gives
the picture brilliance and life.

Collection of Colonel Donald A. Stevning, Indio, California

MARKET DETAIL, OAXACA

Watercolor, 22 x 30 inches, 1971

"The thing that attracted me here was the contrast
of lights and darks. The chicken in the foreground gives
the composition its *whitest* white — the white of the
paper itself. Using this device the other figures are thrown
into the background and a feeling of space
between them is achieved."
"Colors do not separate things," the artist states. "Values do."

HOUSE IN SAN MIGUEL

Watercolor, 27 x 22 inches, 1970

Here the artist was drawn by the attractive doorway
with heaps of broken rocks and the massive bush behind it.
"I made a small compositional layout in pencil.
The flowers, figures, and other incidental details were added
from imagination. When traveling in foreign countries,
it is not usually feasible to spend time painting *in situ*. But
when one has been painting as many years as I have,
he can usually translate a remembered scene to paper from
simple notes of various kinds. Besides, one does not
seek verisimilitude anyway, so a better picture results from
having designed away from the actual scene."

BUSY BROOK

Watercolor, 22 x 27 inches, 1970

This scene in Maine was composed in the studio
from a carefully drawn pencil sketch, made on the spot, in small
size, within the period of a half hour.
"Note," the artist explains, "that there is little variety of color."
Written notes on the side of the sketch reminded
the artist about the colors and values to be used.
The development of certain non-architectural subjects
could then be quite easily done.

BOUGAINVILLEAS, NO. 5

Watercolor, 22 x 30 inches, 1971

"I have always been fascinated by the decorative
appearance of bougainvilleas and have so analyzed their
moods and structure that I can paint them from
imagination alone — without props of any kind. This picture
was so painted. In addition to seeking simple
realism I have striven to present an arrangement decorative
in itself, as the oriental painters do."

WATER SPOUTS

Watercolor, 20 x 30 inches, 1962

"This is a *sky* picture, not a *sea* picture," the artist insists.
"It is a purely imaginary scene. I started with a very low horizon."
Completely from memory he made a small sketch
of an enormous cloud that seemed to fill the sky which he
had seen one afternoon. He recalled a magazine
reproduction of a painting he had seen fifty years before, titled
"Water Spouts in Lisbon Harbor."
His painting became a blend of subject matter, of sea and sky,
with the clouds predominant. This was a spontaneous,
joyous experience, filled with the happy accidentals that create
a memorable work of art.

QUITTING TIME

Watercolor, 21 x 29 inches, 1969

On a drive from Spain to Paris, the Whitakers went
through this quaint village. They took a picture of the groups
of buildings used in the picture painted later
in Whitaker's studio. To give life to the composition, he added
figures and gave them a purpose by the name of the painting.

Collection of Mr. and Mrs. Charles Albert McCann,
Oklahoma City, Oklahoma

RELIC OF THE COMSTOCK ERA

Watercolor, 24 x 21 inches, 1968

Sections cut away from a hill in Virginia City, Nevada,
part of the famous Comstock Lode, inspired this stunning
aquarelle with its glow of warm color
and patterns created by the excavations and the dark
mountain in the background.

FREDERIC WHITAKER, N.A.

UNDER NEW MANAGEMENT

Watercolor, 22 x 30 inches, 1967

The faded or eroded lettering indicates that this
was originally a store that sold charcoal. Traces of charcoal
remain in the refreshment stand which it has
become. Whitaker says he always draws the architectural
parts of the painting first and then asks himself,
"Where do the figures have to be?"

FREDERIC WHITAKER, N.A.

LA ALBERCA DETAIL

Watercolor, 30 x 22 inches, 1969

La Alberca is probably one of the most picturesque
towns in Spain. The age of the buildings and their style of
architecture hold an especial fascination for artists.
Many of the streets are so narrow that the balconies almost
touch. Here the artist has created a strong composition
by using a bold pattern of darks and lights. There is frequently
a depressing drabness found in timeworn districts;
they have been relieved and the atmosphere brightened
by introducing accents of contrived color.

DAY IS DONE

Watercolor, 22 x 30 inches, 1971

When Frederic Whitaker first saw this at night,
he knew he must paint it. The next day he made a sketch in
his studio and that evening returned to the same spot
with campstool and materials to paint, splashing color as
best he could at night. Later he painted it from memory, using
small accents of yellow, red, and orange to define
the direction of the streets and adding other details
for the sake of composition.

CHURCH OF SAN JUAN

Watercolor, 22 x 30 inches, 1948

This church is in the direction of Chapultepec
in the State of Morelos in Mexico. The artist says, "Sometimes
in doing architectural subjects I make the drawings
very carefully with pen and ink or a brush before putting
on the watercolor quite loosely. This way with architectural
realism and the loose composition of watercolor
I achieve the apparent freedom of the whole painting."

Connecticut Watercolor Society, Hartford, 1954

SEVENTEENTH CENTURY RELIC

Watercolor, 30 x 22 inches, 1953

The pink and white aspect of this edifice in
San Miguel de Allende, Mexico, interested the artist. Painted
on the spot, the picture is authentic, a sort of
portrait of a church, mellowed by age. "Incidentally," the
artist notes, "the front entrance of this
church is the one from which the painting FACADE was
adapted many years later."

Hudson Valley Art Association, Hastings-on-Hudson, New York, 1953
DeSaisset Art Museum, University of Santa Clara, 1966

HOLY DAY

Watercolor, 22 x 30 inches, 1971

This was not painted as a portrait but as an impression.
The artist added white doves to light up dark areas. A deep
shadow falling across the foreground pulls the
composition together, gives it a jewel-like quality, and makes
the sunlit figures recede into the background.

THE OLD TOWN AND THE NEW

Watercolor, 22 x 24½ inches, 1964

The patchy quality of this old building in Cascais,
Portugal, and the variations of color in many of the buildings
appealed to the artist. Although a river was
in the background, the artist created a purely imaginary
city rising behind the building.

MUSEUM PIECE

Watercolor, 29 x 21 inches, 1968

Whitaker's affection for ornament was nurtured in his
youth when he worked as an apprentice to a designer in a silver
company. He has never lost interest in it and occasionally
uses *ornament* as the main theme of a watercolor painting.
An outstanding example is this painting in which the artist
displays his great skill as a craftsman and his understanding
of the subject matter. The artist defends ornament
in architecture, declaring: "To be an architect in the past, one
had to be an artist also. Today architecture is more
engineering than art. Without ornament architects have
developed an amazing new style but one must ask if it would
not be even more enchanting if ornament were included in
certain limited areas." This handsome painting offers a
convincing argument in defense of this idea. The intricately
designed piece was discovered in a dark corner of a small room
in the old San Fernando Mission in San Fernando, California.

American Watercolor Society Exhibition, 1968, Herb Olsen Award

ACHIEVEMENTS

AWARDS

Allied Artists of America
American Watercolor Society
Baltimore Watercolor Society
Boston Watercolor Society
Connecticut Watercolor Society
National Academy of Design
National Arts Club
Pennsylvania Academy of Fine Arts
Society of Western Artists
Washington Watercolor Society
Watercolor, U. S. A.

HONORS

American Artists Professional League
    New York
The Artists Fellowship, New York
Audubon Artists, Inc., New York
Philadelphia Watercolor Society

OFFICES HELD

Academic Artists Association
    Advisory board, since 1956
American Amateur Artists Association
    Advisory board, 1952–1965

American Artists Professional League
    Director, 1944–1949
    Vice-President, 1956–1965
American Watercolor Society
    President, 1949–1957
    Director, 1944–46; 1958–1960;
        1961–1963
Audubon Artists, Inc.
    Organizer, 1943
    President, 1943–1946
    Director, 1946–1954
Council of American Artist Societies
    Founder, 1962
    Director, since 1962
Fine Arts Federation of New York
    Director, 1947–1950
International Association of Plastic Arts
    Vice-President, 1954–1961
Municipal Arts Society, New York
    Director, 1946–1950
National Academy of Design
    Vice-President, 1956–1957
    Member of Council, 1953–1956
National Society of Casein Painters
    Director, 1953–1958
Providence Watercolor Society
    Rhode Island
    President, 1934–1937
Village Art Center, New York
    Advisory Board, 1949–1965

Allied Artists of America
American Institute of Fine Arts
American Veterans' Society of Artists
American Watercolor Society
    (Honorary President)
Audubon Artists, Inc.
Council of American Artist Societies
Fine Arts Federation of New York
Fine Arts Guild, San Diego
Kappa Pi National Art Fraternity
    (Honorary)
Knickerbocker Artists
National Academy of Design
    (Academician)
National Society of Casein Painters
National Society of Mural Painters
    (Honorary)
Royal Society of Arts, Britain
    (Fellow)
San Diego Watercolor Society
Society of Western Artists
Watercolor West
West Coast Watercolor Society

WRITINGS

Books —
Whitaker on Watercolor
    Reinhold Publishing Co., 1963
Guide to Painting Better Pictures
    Reinhold Publishing Co., 1965

Magazines —
American Artist
    Contributing Editor since 1956
The Artist (London)
Today's Art

FEATURED IN PUBLICATIONS

Books —
Award Winning Art
    Margaret Harold
    Allied Publications, 1965
Contemporary Authors
Frederic Whitaker
    Janice Lovoos
    Northland Press, 1972
Fundamentals of Watercolor Painting
    Watson-Guptill, 1970
History of American Watercolor Society
    Ralph Fabri
    The Guinn Co., Inc.
Twenty-Four Watercolorists
    Norman Kent and Susan Meyer
    (unreleased)
Watercolor Demonstrated
    Ernest W. Watson and Norman Kent
    Watson-Guptill, 1945
Watercolor Methods
    Norman Kent
    Watson-Guptill, 1945
100 Watercolor Techniques
    Norman Kent
    Watson-Guptill, 1968
Who's Who in America
Who's Who in Art
Who's Who in the West

Magazines —
American Artist
The Artist (London)
Caravan
Design
The Pan American
Revue Moderne (Paris)
Today's Art

MUSEUM PRESENTATIONS

Museum of Fine Arts, Boston
Hispanic Museum, New York
I. B. M. Collection
Metropolitan Museum of Art
National Academy of Design
National Arts Club
Abilene, Texas
Albion, Michigan
Atchison, Kansas
Auburn, New York
Canton, New York
Columbus, Mississippi
Granville, Ohio
Hickory, North Carolina
Huntington, Long Island, New York

Lakeland, Florida
Newark, New Jersey
New Britain, Connecticut
New Haven, Connecticut
Norfolk, Virginia
Pocatello, Idaho
Providence, Rhode Island
Reading, Pennsylvania
Salt Lake City, Utah
Seattle, Washington
Southhampton, Long Island, New York
Springfield, Massachusetts
Syracuse, New York
Tamassee, North Carolina
Terre Haute, Indiana
Wichita, Kansas

THIS BOOK
WAS DESIGNED BY ROBERT JACOBSON
AND SET IN 12-POINT CALEDONIA
WITH PERPETUA TITLING.
IT WAS PRINTED ON WEYCROFT TEXT
AT NORTHLAND PRESS
AND BOUND AT ROSWELL BINDERY.